NEW GROUND

NEW GROUND

WESTERN AMERICAN NARRATIVE
AND THE LITERARY CANON

A. CARL BREDAHL, JR.

THE UNIVERSITY OF NORTH CAROLINA PRESS

Chapel Hill | London

Library of Congress Cataloging-in-Publication Data

Bredahl, A. Carl (Axel Carl), 1940–

New ground : western American narrative and the literary canon /
A. Carl Bredahl, Jr.
p.   cm.   Bibliography: p.
Includes index.   ISBN 0-8078-1854-2 (alk. paper)
1. American literature—West (U.S.)—History and criticism.
2. American literature—Middle West—History and criticism.
3. Western stories—History and criticism. 4. West (U.S.) in
literature. 5. Middle West in literature. 6. Narration
(Rhetoric) 7. Canon (Literature) I. Title.
PS271.B74   1989   88-38938   813'.54'093278—dc 19   CIP

Portions of several chapters have appeared elsewhere in
different form: the discussion of *My Lady Pokahontas* from
Chapter 1 appeared as "Responding to the 'Airplant' Tradition:
John Cook's *My Lady Pokahontas*," in *Southern Literary Journal*
21, no. 1 (Fall 1988): 54–63; a section of Chapter 3
appeared as " 'The Young Thing Within': Divided Narrative
and Sherwood Anderson's *Winesburg, Ohio*" in *Midwest Quarterly*
(Summer 1986): 422–37; a shorter version of Chapter 4 appeared
as "The Body as Matrix: Narrative Pattern in *Green Hills of
Africa*" in *Midwest Quarterly* (Summer 1987): 455–72; and
Chapter 8 appeared as "The Outsider as Sexual Center:
Wright Morris and the Integrated Imagination" in *Studies in
the Novel* (Spring 1986): 66–73. The author is grateful for
permission to reproduce this material.

The paper in this book meets the guidelines for permanence
and durability of the Committee on Production Guidelines
for Book Longevity of the Council on Library Resources.

Manufactured in the United States of America

93 92 91 90 89   5 4 3 2 1

For William R. Robinson

Contents

Preface

Reconsideration of accepted literary assumptions has generated so much interest in recent years that articles on the debate have begun appearing in national newspapers. The *New York Times* has run several, one of the most recent being James Atlas's "On Campus: The Battle of the Books" (June 5, 1988). Academic debate in the popular press should not be surprising because the implications extend—as they properly should—far beyond the classroom. Many recognize that the discussion has significant political implications and angrily decry such reconsiderations, framing their argument in the language of God and country in order to cast aspersions on the whole endeavor. Their fears are valid; those whose interest lies in maintaining the status quo recognize that challenge to the literary establishment does more than question which books are read in college courses. It challenges fundamental assumptions of the society.

New Ground is part of the reconsideration. For the political reasons just indicated, I do not desire to see noncanonical works simply brought into the canon, an action that would only reinforce the power of those defining the canon. Rather, I would like to see the canon broken open by imaginations that violate the assumptions built into the whole idea of a canon. Reconsideration of America's accepted body of literary work usually involves focusing attention on the writings of ethnic and women writers. My interest, however, lies in western writers, an interest developed out of the sense that in the American West an imagination exists that respects surface. Beginning with respect for the surfaces of the land and moving to respect for surfaces of those whose lives are interdependent with the land, the western imagination offers a healthy corrective to a culture that too often distrusts surfaces it cannot force into conformity with previous assumptions. My effort in the text that follows is to establish the distinction in values between the products of traditional (canonical) imaginations and those of western imaginations.

The preparation of *New Ground* has gone through more stages than I care to remember. The text of the following pages bears little resemblance to that of a manuscript begun several years ago as a study of energy in the American imagination. I indicate in the Introduction that much of the shift came as a result of Fulbright lectureships in Pakistan and India, where I was given the opportunity to rethink my assumptions about American literature. I am particularly grateful, therefore, to the Exchange of Scholars Program.

My colleagues have offered me appreciated encouragement, reading and commenting on much of the manuscript. I most sincerely want to thank Richard Brantley, Ira Clark, Melvyn New, John Perlette, and Eldon Turner for their ready and generous support. During the last year, David Leverenz, who spent many hours talking with me and reading the manuscript, offered help that was invaluable.

My thanks also to Marie A. Nelson, who typed early sections of the manuscript, and Deanna Nesbitt, whose work on the final text was an enormous help. I would also like to acknowledge and thank Brenda W. Kolb, Sandra Eisdorfer, and Iris Tillman Hill of the University of North Carolina Press for their considered advice and conscientious work.

For the pleasure of discussion with new friends at the conventions of the Western Literature Association, I am grateful and wish to underscore how important their ideas have been.

This work was written to appeal to the general reader as well as to the student and the specialist. Accordingly, I present the scholarly apparatus as simply as possible. Secondary works that are quoted in the text correspond to complete references in the notes. However, I have chosen not to clutter the text with numerous page references for quotations from the fictional works that are discussed in detail and at length. In these instances, I more informally direct the reader to the

approximate location of a quoted passage in the original work. I believe that this method provides a text that is more readable yet no less
instructive.

And finally but not least, my wife, Susan, as she has for the past
twenty years, always supported with her quiet strength my often dis-
quieting efforts. Thank you.

Introduction

In the fall of 1982 I accepted a position as senior Fulbright lecturer in India. My assignment—to lecture on American thought and writing, to describe the direction and characteristics of the American imagination, and to work with individual instances of its expression—was not unlike that asked of me on my return to the United States: "Tell us something about Indian writing!" "What kind of fiction does India produce?" "How does Indian narrative compare with American?"

Overseas, of course, I had asked myself those same questions, but I found answers difficult to come by. Instead of *an* Indian imagination, there were many, too many to get hold of in a few months. Focusing on one necessarily meant neglecting others. Much of western Europe and the United States, for example, chooses to know the India of Paul Scott, David Lean, or E. M. Forster, all native Englishmen; less frequently do we know the India of R. K. Narayan and Salman Rushdie, native Indians who work in English. To ask about the India of Khushwant Singh (a Sikh of the Punjab), Tagore (a Hindu from Bengal), or Iqbal (a Muslim claimed by both Pakistan and India) usually elicits blank stares. And yet another India is discovered in the writing from southern India; its language and culture traced to Dravidian rather than Arian roots, this region takes pride in its distinct differences from Delhi—as, for that matter, does the Punjab, Kashmir, and Assam. Diversity has been much of the fascination of India for centuries, and, not unexpectedly, narrative diversity is part of that wealth.

I begin *New Ground* with this reference to India because my all too brief experience on the subcontinent caused me to rethink my assumptions concerning American values generally and, more particularly, *the* American imagination as expressed in the traditional American literary canon. Presenting a single imagination to a culture different from my own was relatively easy to do. Few questioned my authority, and indeed I had been trained to understand that the American literary experience, with variations, was essentially unified—was in fact synonymous with that of the East Coast. Every country has its literary power center, and the East is America's. Certainly the major publishers are there, effectively forcing writers to come to terms with their demands. But the economic and cultural energies of the United States also center in the East, attracting the outsiders—the Garlands, Twains, Dreisers, Cathers, Hemingways, Fitzgeralds, Pounds, and Eliots.

As academics, many of us who went to East or West Coast graduate schools (and significantly, I think, to *English* departments) work with *an* American experience because we have been trained to focus on that body of writing valued by the East. Though New England has always been the heart of this traditional orientation, some critics, like Lewis Simpson, define the southern experience of alienation as interrelating with and finally replacing New England's "City on a Hill." *New Ground* suggests that this commitment to the traditional canon, a commitment stemming initially from a combination of inherited European expectations and New World conditions, has been self-perpetuating and that the fascination with the "New England Mind"—albeit frequently a troubled fascination—so dominates the literary expectations of both writers and critics that responses to alternative imaginative expressions are thereby diminished. Central to this eastern imagination, I argue, is concern with the problems and possibilities inherent in the act of intellectually enclosing wilderness. The eastern imagination generates a story fascinated by mind and intellectual energy, a mind fundamentally distrustful of space.

Charles Olson begins his *Call Me Ishmael* (1947) with these words: "I take SPACE to be the central fact to man born in America, from Folsom cave to now. I spell it large because it comes large here. Large, and without mercy." I also take space to be the central fact for the American imagination but wish to distinguish between responses that distrust and those that embrace the demands of space. Like Richard Poirier in a later study, *A World Elsewhere*, Olson perceives a singularly American response, which he defines in terms of enclosure: "So if you want to know why Melville nailed us in *Moby-Dick*, consider whaling. Consider whaling as FRONTIER, and INDUSTRY. A product wanted, men got it: big business. The Pacific as sweatshop. Man, led, against the biggest damndest creature nature uncorks. The whaleship as factory, the whaleboat the precision instrument." Converting the largest of creatures into a commercial product is the most physical instance of enclosing wilderness, and one at the heart of *Moby-Dick*.

Herman Melville explored what became for him the appalling contrast between his lived experience in "wilderness" and the confines of his social environment. Each attracted and horrified; each offered support and threatened destruction. Tommo and Taji, the central figures in the early novels *Typee* and *Mardi*, are motivated by their desire to break free from constricting physical and mental enclosures; they find, however, that their new freedom leads only to new enclosures. When Taji attempts his own version of lighting out for the territories at the end of *Mardi*, it is essentially an act of desperation—"Now, I am my own soul's emperor; and my first act is abdication!" These two protagonists sought the imagined freedom of literal new worlds, but narrators in Melville's later work reject that impulse and find themselves working within the social structures from which their earlier counterparts had sought to escape. It is not, therefore, until the pivotal *White-Jacket* that Melville hits his stride, creating for the first time a narrator that works within a known and tightly framed cultural construct, in this case the USS *Neversink*. The brilliance of his next novel, *Moby-Dick*, in part results from restricting the narrative imagination to the self-contained world of the *Pequod*. After *Moby-Dick*—in *Pierre*, "Bartleby, the Scrivener," "Benito Cereno," "The Encantadas," and *The Confidence Man*—enclosures become increasingly constrictive. And Melville deals, finally, in *Billy Budd, Sailor*, with the political realities of the fact that enclosure, not wilderness, is the major given of our lives.[1]

My description of an eastern preoccupation with enclosure extends to southern as well as northern writing, even though I am aware that the usual perception of the South seems to contradict my statement about intellectually enclosing wilderness.[2] We think of the southern mind as one for which "urban" and "intellectual" are fighting words to be contrasted with the Southerner's commitment to body, senses, and land. But in this regard Lewis Simpson's argument in *The Dispossessed Garden* becomes instructive, because he points to concerns common to both the North and the South—as did Perry Miller in *Errand into the Wilderness* and Richard Beale Davis in *Intellectual Life in the Colonial South, 1585–1763*.

What Simpson, Miller, and Davis implicitly recognize is an effort along the entire eastern coast to extend and protect the socially sacred from the onslaught of cultural or physical wilderness. In the North, the myths of a City on a Hill and Manifest Destiny are intellectual constructs perceived as necessary to the rest of the world. The southern myth—and here both Miller and Davis begin their arguments with the early historian Samuel Purchas—is Edenic, the myth of a beautiful world eventually threatened by an urban mentality and protected by southern gentility. Common to both myths is their creation out of a European longing which looked to the New World for physical and spiritual haven. One might in fact argue that the commercial base underlying eastern economies was itself the product of European dreams, with both northern and southern colonies perceiving the land and its products as material to be reshaped, packaged, and sold to an awaiting Europe.

The literature of the traditional American canon—Edenic in the South, nationalistic in the North—expresses this uncomfortable fascination and concern with enclosure. The main body of my text argues that while a troubled fascination with enclosure generated many of America's greatest works, its assumptions came to so dominate our expectations that we frequently fail to appreciate literary expressions that do not define themselves through enclosure. These other works, it seems to me, develop out of fascination rather than discomfort with space and therefore present significantly different narrative and structural demands. I certainly agree with Charles Olson that space is the central fact to man born in America but maintain that the imaginations making up the traditional canon confront space by converting it into salable commodities, units of known value. However, that need not be and is not the only response to the fact of space in America.

The land-based economies of the Great Plains, in contrast to the commercial economies of the East, grew out of lives dependent upon the land and subject to its whims and characteristics. Confronting an environment of extravagant size, weather, and configuration, the western imagination had finally to discard assumptions of imposing self and enclosing landscape, efforts that in the West met inevitably with disaster. While the South, both a slave and a land-based economy, could impose tobacco and cotton on its lands for economic and political as well as environmental reasons, the West did not have the luxury of that dominating stance. Farmers and ranchers ultimately had to ask what the land would tolerate. What therefore developed in the place of the effort to impose and reshape was the perception of the need to realign assumptions about an individual's relation to the land. Much western writing is the story of that realignment.

In recent years, in books like *Reconstructing American Literature*, feminist and ethnic writers have presented alternatives to a white male literature. A case also needs to be made for recognizing that continued defining of the canon in terms of enclosure implicitly rejects works with different formal structures, whether or not they were written by white males. Anne Bradstreet, Emily Dickinson, and Sylvia Plath, for example, depend on enclosure for the strength of their poetry; I believe they do so because of their eastern backgrounds and consequent assumptions. On the other hand, few students of American literature read Harvey Fergusson or Frank Waters or Ivan Doig, and many have misread, I think, Ernest Hemingway and Hamlin Garland.[3]

I am intrigued by several facts: one of twentieth-century America's most characteristic forms—that evidenced in *Winesburg, Ohio*—is accorded no name, almost as though we preferred to think that the form did not exist; Hemingway's *Green Hills of Africa*, a central work from the writer's period of greatest productivity, is slighted by every critic of his work; and Harvey Fergusson's *The Conquest of Don Pedro* (1954), described by several students of southwestern writing as one of the finest pieces to come from that region, is no longer in print. These are scattered instances of what happens when a particular approach to literature dominates and determines the canon, but they should alert readers of American literature to the possibility that new discoveries await our attention.

The writings I focus on are all products of some of the most respected western and midwestern writers in twentieth-century America. At the same time, they offer diversity of time, region, and form.

With that same concern for diversity, I conclude this study with an examination of the western movies of John Ford and Sam Peckinpah. Thus I am able to apply my argument to narratives of a second medium, where different approaches to the genre illustrate the strengths and techniques of imaginations fascinated in one instance with enclosure and in the other with space. To value only one—John Ford is typically preferred by traditional audiences—is to miss the qualities and challenges of the other.

Recently, when I described to a colleague some of the works I had come across in researching this study, he remarked that he had long been convinced that academics had yet to discover America. As an academic, I am made uncomfortable by such a comment, but I must admit that he verbalized what I had come to feel. And it is what many students have also found to be true—there are many American works of impressive quality to which too few of us have had access and which await our discovery. What follows is part of my effort at discovery.

I

Working within Enclosure:
The Traditional Canon

Within the College Yard, its elements and items gain presence by what
has been done (little as it is, of enclosure—with a glance at the
old misery!) and how I may put it that the less "good" thing enclosed,
approached, *defined*, often looks better than the less good thing
not enclosed, not defined, not approached.

The Notebooks of Henry James

In December 1904, Henry James returned to Harvard for a visit. Several notations made in his notebooks at the time indicate that he paid particular attention to the Yard and its wall: "I noted for my recall 'The Gates—questions of the Gates and of the fact of *enclosure* and of disclosure in general—the so importunate American question (of Disclosure—call it so!) above all.' " Thinking then of Cambridge and Oxford, he remembered how their "grilles" have the "admirable office of making things look *interesting*—make so—by their intervention."[1] For James enclosure provides definition, placing in sharp focus an object's essential interest. Thus "enclosure" becomes an effective method of disclosing, one more effective than the "importunate American" tendency to disclose by simply pouring forth. Narratively, James discloses by enclosing, placing romantic ideals within enclosing social relationships. He thereby gives definition and his particular sense of "interest" to those ideals.[2]

Equally characteristic of enclosure is its protective aspect, and as college freshmen are traditionally seen to need protection from urban wiles (and wilds), James's appreciation of enclosure appropriately focuses on the Harvard Gates, for the Yard encloses the freshmen dormitories. The protective value of enclosure was important to much of early America, where physical wilderness or individual aggressiveness threatened settlement. Consequently, the New World adventure was comprehended—and thereby enclosed—within a preconceived intellectual framework.[3] Some settlers, like the seventeenth-century Thomas Morton, undoubtedly felt that the New World offered release from Old World oppression, but for most, security depended upon conforming to an idea rather than experiencing a wilderness.[4] True "freedom," argued John Winthrop, deputy governor of the Massachusetts Bay Colony in a 1645 speech before the General Court, could only be found in the restraints of "civil," rather than in the licentiousness of "natural," liberty.

William Spengemann has demonstrated that the earliest European explorers found it crucial to see the New World as an extension of the Old rather than as a place of unbounded freedom. In his reading of the letters of Christopher Columbus, Spengemann provides ample evidence that the discovery of a genuinely new continent threatened contemporary religious assumptions concerning a global geography based on the Holy Trinity:

> As the disorderly facts break through Columbus's elegantly simple view of the world, suggesting the existence of a totally unknown continent, a flood of unwelcome yet subtly exhilarating consequences threaten to pour through the crumbling walls of his belief. . . . Evidence of an unauthorized continent would only get him into trouble at home, for the authorities were, if anything, even less prepared than Columbus to entertain the notion of inhabited lands outside the island of earth. So Columbus retreats once again from the suggestion, back into the safer confines of authorized belief. . . . Columbus's letter projects the image of a self so dependent on home, finally, and on the beliefs which home represents, that it cannot possibly adapt to the disruptive facts it encounters. . . . Both the strategic demands of his argument and the psychological demands of his self-image determine that when expectations and experiences come into conflict he shall opt for his prior beliefs.[5]

Narratively and psychologically, Columbus resists the wilderness by rhetorically enclosing his experience within previously understood frameworks.

Those who followed Columbus maintained his enclosing stance toward the New World. The imagination of early America perceived the New World as fulfilling Old World dreams, whether defined as the

City on a Hill or a potential garden. Both a New Englander like Nathaniel Ward and a southerner like Samuel Purchas, it should be remembered, viewed the new land in Edenic terms. Richard Beale Davis describes the vision of Purchas:

> "Virginia's Verger" . . . is a well-reasoned argument for greater expansion in North America, including high moral reasons for taking land from the Indians. . . . Then he proceeds to justify colonization by right of discovery and settlement. Virginia, he tells his reader, is a vast, rich Eden waiting to supply living space for the poor of England. National defense, through advanced bases far removed from mother England, is an argument as relevant for our time as his, and between the two periods early southerners used it to justify all sorts of actions, especially frontier land-grabbing: "Now is our Seed-time. . . . God goeth before us. . . ."
> Thus reasoned the English mind in the old age of Elizabeth and the whole reign of James I. Hakluyt and Purchas epitomize British attitudes towards North America, especially its southern coast, for almost all the seventeenth century and to some extent down through the first settlement of Georgia in the 1730s. Thus reasoned many or most of those who had ventured across the Atlantic themselves and who were quoted by the two geographers.[6]

Davis is certainly correct when later he distinguishes between the southerner who saw his world as a "tropical paradise" and the northerner who spoke of "howling wilderness," but both perceptions necessitate enclosing the physical landscape: the southerner must convert it, the northerner wall it out.

Crucial to these early imaginations was the Jamesian valuing of enclosure, the perception that only within intellectual definitions or physical structures could possibility be explored and realized. In these terms we understand William Bradford's presentation of tiny Plymouth as part of historical forces stretching back to antiquity and St. Jean de Crèvecoeur's struggles to withstand the potential anarchy of a moral forest.

Many eastern writings are grounded within the assumptions of enclosure. Nathaniel Ward's *Simple Cobbler of Aggawam* (1647) details with pride the efforts of the few short years that brought forth the towns and lands of the new colonies. William Byrd's *History of the Dividing Line*, written in 1728 and one of the earliest major southern works, features an unusual protagonist, a survey line. Byrd and his companions struggle through the forest and swamp of the Virginia/North Carolina border, pushing the line that will divide what the aristocratic Byrd sees as the civilization of Virginia from the crudity and the chaotic wilderness of North Carolina. In all these writings, both the garden of Virginia and the New England City on a Hill were to be protected, explored, and extended within a variety of narrative enclosures.[7]

In both prose and poetry, the Puritan sought the protection and possibility of language just as he sought to place his life within the protection and possibility of God's plan.[8] Puritan histories, therefore, see local events within sweeping time spans, and Puritan diaries are predicated on a shaped and providential universe. Poetry provided a particularly tight verbal structure within which an individual—like Edward Taylor—could explore his life/Life.[9] Given rhetorical freedom, which would linguistically parallel John Winthrop's natural liberty, the individual might wander helplessly in verbal wilderness. But poetry has form, and like God's plan, that form sustains and encourages growth.

In prose, the protection offered by poetry's structure found expression in the safety provided by traditional rhetorical patterns. Sermons and diaries are the best-known instances of Puritan prose, but captivity narratives, one of the earliest and most enduring prose forms to appear in America, also relied on pattern for safety. Captivity narratives recount the ordeals of colonists captured by Indians and forced to endure physical and mental hardship before being returned to God's Colony. Richard Slotkin's discussion of these narratives emphasizes the importance of their formally tight structures: "Both the captivity and the hunter mythologies see the frontier experience as one of regression: civilized men and women leave contemporary society, and enter—willingly or as captives—a primitive, primal world. If they can maintain their racial/cultural integrity in that world, if they can seize the natural, original power that is immanent in that world, and if they can defeat the forces that seek to prevent their return to civilization, then on their return they will be capable of renewing the moral and physical powers of the society they originally left."[10]

Slotkin stresses the salvational need to capture and defeat the wilderness that attempts to make them captives. Captivity narratives seem to describe the effort to avoid capture by the unknown; more to the point, however, the effort is to remain captured by the known—these are, as their name indicates, narratives of captivity, not of liberation. Because the narratives are written after the event, successful completion of Slotkin's conditional clauses is accomplished rhetorically. Captivity narrative becomes, therefore, a verbal strategy for testing and controlling the horrors of the wilderness.

The most famous of the captivity narratives is that of Mary Rowlandson, a minister's wife taken in the winter of 1675 and held for almost three months. In writing of those events, Rowlandson gives prominence to the word *remove* as a descriptive term in the titles for each section of her narrative. She views her capture by the wilderness as a series of removes from the security of her known world. As a counter to that sequence of removes, Rowlandson attempts to use language to distance herself from the physical experience, establishing the possibility of verbal removes from the unknown. Language thus provides an enclosure within which Rowlandson explores the threat to her safety.

The narrative begins with a description of the Indians' arrival, a description strikingly reserved in language and syntax:

> On the tenth of February 1675, Came the Indians with great numbers upon Lancaster: Their first coming was about Sunrising; hearing the noise of some Guns, we looked out; several Houses were burning, and the Smoke ascending to Heaven. There were five persons taken in one house, the Father, and the Mother and a sucking Child, they knockt on the head; the other two they took and carried away alive. There were two others, who being out of their Garison upon some occasion were set upon; one was knockt on the head, the other escaped: Another their [sic] was who running along was shot and wounded, and fell down; he begged of them his life, promising them Money (as they told me) but they would not hearken to him but knockt him in head, and stript him naked, and split open his Bowels.[11]

The final sentence presents a grisly picture, but even so the narrative stance is matter of fact. Sentences state rather than exclaim; instead of reacting to the situation, Rowlandson presents it as an observer. The detachment is maintained until the end of the first paragraph, when Rowlandson calls the Indians "murtherous wretches"; only in that term does she offer a comment on the events.

But the experience will not allow the description to remain de-
tached. As the Indians near her house and events touch her family,
Rowlandson's emotions rise and her images become increasingly
vivid:

> Now is the dreadfull hour come, that I have often heard of (in
> time of War, as it was the case of others) but now mine eyes see
> it. Some in our house were fighting for their lives, others wal-
> lowing in their blood, the House on fire over our heads, and the
> bloody Heathen ready to knock us on the head, if we stirred
> out. . . . But out we must go, the fire increasing, and coming
> along behind us, roaring, and the Indians gaping before us with
> their Guns, Spears and Hatchets to devour us.

The initial linguistic detachment diminishes as physical horror drives
the narrator from the security of her known world, but that initial verbal reserve points to the captive's attempt to defend against what her
eyes see. In this instance even the "devour us" is clearly more biblical,
and therefore more interpretive, than realistic. The technique through
which the narrative sometimes achieves detachment—images stripped
of personal emotional value—defuses threat.

The Indians hold her, but the narrator works at trying to enclose
them within her rational paradigm of God's providential universe.
Turning her eyes to the Bible, Rowlandson seeks to block out wilderness. Christian language orders the confusion of being forced by savages to move from place to place without knowing her destination
or the duration of her imprisonment, forced by cold and hunger to
seek comfort from strangers. Scripture clarifies and places experience
within an overall, purposeful plan. Rowlandson thus transforms her
amazement at the sight of the butchered Puritans into amazement at
God's awesome power:

> There was one who was chopt into the head with a Hatchet, and
> stript naked, and yet was crawling up and down. It is a solemn
> sight to see so many Christians lying in their blood, some here,
> and some there, like a company of Sheep torn by Wolves, All of
> them stript naked by a company of hell-hounds, roaring, sing-
> ing, ranting, and insulting, as if they would have torn our very
> hearts out; yet the Lord by His Almighty power preserved a
> number of us from death.

This ordering of events, of course, comes after the fact, in stepping
back and reflecting. That distinction is important, because during

those moments when Indians literally surround her, their confusing numbers and erratic movements confound her senses, her reason, and her heart. Experience breaks in and disorders intention. The Indians are "thick as trees," surrounding her with what seem to be "a thousand Hatchets going at once." Later, "sitting alone in the midst" of "a numerous crew of Pagans," she loses her emotional resolve and weeps in their presence. Only thoughts of God can still the image. Through the Word and her words, she surrounds those who surround her.

In *Regeneration through Violence*, Richard Slotkin suggests that part of the power of the captivity narrative comes from the reader's titillated interest in wondering how intimately the captive ventures into wilderness, the extent to which he or she participates in savagery. When Rowlandson describes herself taking a "tough and sinewy" piece of boiled horse foot from an English child who "lay sucking, gnawing, chewing and slabbering of it in the mouth and hand," Slotkin says that the narrator "feels herself metamorphosed into a beast, a wilderness thing."[12] But the participles of the description associate the child, rather than the narrator, with the dancing, yelling, whooping Indians. The narrator justifies her action with a quote from Job that transforms the "abomination" into "pleasant refreshing." Similarly, while she shows herself eating a half-cooked horse liver, "with the blood about my mouth," she quotes Scripture, transforming the act from "bitter" to "sweet" and mitigating the savage image of herself.

Finally, when Rowlandson moves to reunion with her community, the intellectual and religious enclosure of her condition as a civilized captive takes literal shape. Friends and family replace the Indians who once surrounded her. When this happens, images suddenly lose that visual immediacy they had in the wilderness, becoming scriptural and metaphorical:

> I remember in the night season, how the other day I was in the midst of thousands of enemies, and nothing but death before me: It is then hard work to perswade my self, that ever I should be satisfied with bread again. But now we are fed with the finest of the Wheat, and, as I may say, With honey out of the rock: In stead of the Husk, we have the fatted Calf: The thoughts of these things in the particulars of them, and of the love and goodness of God towards us, make it true of me, what David said of himself, Psal. 6. 5. *I watered my Couch with my tears.*

Safe at last from the concrete experience of horror, wanting to believe that Providence does prevail, and calmed by familiar sights, the narrator can reflect rather than look at blood. "The finest of the Wheat . . . honey out of the rock . . . the fatted Calf" were in short supply at seventeenth-century Massachusetts Bay; idealized images, therefore, shut out those experiences that had been graphic and tangible. Having narratively completed her "remove," Rowlandson imagines that she can "stand still and see" experience as "a shadow, a blast, a bubble, and things of no continuance." Standing astonished by God rather than by the Indians, she makes God her captor and turns her eyes from the vain sights of this world and toward the images of the Christian myth. As wilderness images disappear from the story, the Christian captive lives through her effort to make things unseen enclose experiential horror. It is important, however, to stress the effort she must make in restoring enclosing rhetorical patterns to an experience that continually threatens to violate those patterns. At the end of her narrative, she finds that sleep no longer comes easily, but whether because of a new awe for the power of God which others only take for granted or because she has seen horrors she cannot control we will never know.

The commitment of the imagination to exploring within the givens of enclosure generates the widely recognized strength of traditional American literature. Seeing a natural wilderness that must be converted into gardens, this imagination seeks to realize inner potential. In the North, James and Hawthorne extend the Puritan John Winthrop's argument that only within constraints can the individual be truly free. Hester Prynne, for example, gains in stature and strength as she remains in Salem; Daisy Miller, for all her youthful freshness, is naive; Isabel Archer finds her greatest reach within herself; and Lambert Strether, the apparent exception who proves the rule, moves from denial to acceptance of life's possibilities within a structured society. All are stories of freedom discovered as part of, in Winthrop's terms, a civil environment. Even Melville's Ahab, one might argue, becomes demonic to the extent that he resists enclosure.

In Hawthorne and James, enclosure becomes a means through which one can explore those human capabilities that distinguish him from the natural world. Similarly, the South values the protective form of enclosure expressed in the Edenic myth. William Byrd and Robert Beverly gave early expression to this myth, which by its nature defends a fixed environment. Change is anathema to Eden, and consequently the organic properties of the very land treasured by the South threaten the myth. Ironically, therefore, the southern myth, which theoretically idealized physical environment over northern acquisitive desires, is strikingly intangible. In fact, one critic has described nineteenth-century southern writing as "airplant" literature, literature that receives none of its sustenance from direct contact with the soil.[13]

Though early American colonies were called "plantations" (or plantings), southern plantings disregarded the soil and were based on assumptions similar to those informing William Byrd's effort to draw a line around the Virginia garden. Only in walling out wilderness, sloth, and sexuality could civilization grow—*History of the Dividing Line*, we must remember, was Byrd's public effort, not his private indulgence. Thus a striking number of scenes in nineteenth-century southern writing take place indoors, where individuals talk endlessly about social or economic problems. When scenes do occur outdoors, they often evoke little sense of physical place.[14]

William Gilmore Simms's *The Yemassee* (1835) provides a good example of the enclosed (or "airplant") world of southern writing because much of its action occurs outdoors and it therefore seems to contradict what I have just said. Set in the early eighteenth century in the area that was to become South Carolina, *The Yemassee* is the story of conflict between white settlers and the Yemassee Indians. Though the novel takes place almost entirely in the physical wilderness, we rarely see that world and then only in the most generalized terms. The story opens with a central figure, the old Indian chief Sanutee, moving through the woods:

> Without further pause or inquiry, Sanutee turned, and taking his way through the body of the town, soon gained the river. Singling forth a canoe, hollowed out from a cypress, and which lay with an hundred others drawn up upon the miry bank, he succeeded with little exertion in launching it forth into the water . . . He paddled himself directly across the river, though then somewhat swollen and impetuous from a recent and heavy freshet. Carefully concealing his canoe in a clustering shelter of sedge and cane, which grew along the banks, he took his way,

still closely followed by his faithful dog, into the bosom of a forest much more dense than that which he had left, and which
promised a better prospect of the game which he desired.

The passage speaks of "river" and "forest" and "freshet," but it might
be any river or forest. Cypress, sedge, and cane are mentioned, but
Sanutee's canoe is not drawn from a particular cypress.

We should not be surprised, therefore, at the author's willingness to
pass over opportunities for description. For example, when the hero
Gabriel Harrison runs along the river at one point in the story, we
focus on his thoughts rather than on what he sees. And when Bess
Matthews, the love interest, walks into the woods that harbor the
rattlesnake she will later encounter, the setting could as well be England or southern France or almost anyplace:

> The scene itself, to the eye, was of character to correspond har-
> moniously with the song of birds and the playful sport of zeph-
> yrs. The rich green of the leaves—the deep crimson of the wild
> flower—the gemmed and floral-knotted long grass that carpeted
> the path—the deep, solemn shadows of evening, and the trees
> through which the now declining sun was enabled only here
> and there to sprinkle a few drops from his golden censer—all
> gave power to that spell of quiet.

The scene presents itself "to the eye" but without any specific object
that can be seen. Thus if one wishes to speak of *The Yemassee* as a novel
that takes place in the natural world, he is hard-pressed to find passages supporting that contention.

As the physical world of *The Yemassee* is enclosed in an imagined
environment, so also is the novel's plot. Commentators have frequently remarked on Simms's presenting the Indians as people rather
than stereotypical savages. Simms certainly takes time with his descriptions of Indian domestic life, but his interest lies less in realism
than in the fact that these eighteenth-century Indians are threatened
with losing the same Eden that nineteenth-century southern whites
have come to value. Sanutee and the Indians who follow him fight
for a world that the whites want to win for themselves. Other novels
of Indian confrontation would present the old chief Sanutee as the
villain. In *The Yemassee*, however, the cruelties Sanutee instigates are
mitigated by the fact that he is defending against his way of life being
taken from him.

Thus Simms's interest in the Indians lies not in the realistic presentation of their way of life but in the ideals they fight to preserve. Whether or not Matiwan, Sanutee's squaw, would really talk back to her husband as she does in the novel is not an issue. What is central to the stories of Sanutee, Matiwan, their son Occonestoga, and the love of Gabriel Harrison and Bess Matthews is the common purity of their ideals. Sanutee fights for the life that once belonged to the Yemassee, disowning Occonestoga, who has become a drunkard. When Occonestoga is killed, it is in a forest grove to which Simms gives religious value: "The whole scene was unique in that solemn grandeur, that sombre hue, that deep spiritual repose, in which the human imagination delights to invest the region which has been rendered remarkable for the deed of punishment or crime. . . . The ancient oak, a bearded Druid, was there to contribute to the due solemnity of all associations." And equally pure is Bess: "And she was there—the girl of seventeen—confiding, yet blushing at her own confidence, with an affection as warm as it was unqualified and pure." *The Yemassee*, then, is a novel portraying not physical reality but a world of ideals and purity. The strength of the Yemassee lies in their struggle for their once beautiful world. The commitment of Gabriel Harrison—and the southern imagination—is to maintaining that beauty in the future.

After the Civil War, southerners could no longer commit themselves to a present or future Eden. It is not surprising, therefore, to find John Esten Cooke, an important southern writer both before and after the war, creating a narrator who looks back to an idealized love. The book is *My Lady Pokahontas* (1879) and the narrator a Puritan soldier named Anas Todkill. Turning from an immediate reality to the days of earliest settlement is only part of the effort in Cooke's narrative; the story he chooses is that most romantic of southern legends, the romance of Captain John Smith and Pocahontas. Cooke shapes the love affair to emphasize past glories, the lovely maid and chivalric hero, a troubled present, and an adoring narrator. The story is therefore appropriate to both postwar southern values and the more generalized commitment to a protecting myth.

My Lady Pokahontas is presented by Anas Todkill, a first-person narrator who serves as observer to the lovers. Like the world of William Faulkner's Caddy Compson (who, according to Faulkner, is too beautiful to narrate her own story), the world shared by Captain Smith and

Pocahontas must remain separated from that of the reader, a world to be talked about but not touched—thus the use of the adoring narrator. Todkill sees his captain as the ultimate heroic figure, worthy of complete admiration, and the narrative stance is appropriate to a myth-oriented society that sees the male as the guardian of both cultivated values and lovely women. Todkill introduces and closes Captain Smith's part in the story by associating Captain Smith with the heroes (significantly, both the historical and the tragical) of Shakespeare. And it is certainly in those terms that Todkill sees the founder of Jamestown.

As perceived by this imagination, the introduction of Pocahontas, the embodiment of the land, has none of the wanton qualities sometimes attributed to her: "The angel comes out of the woods with her wild train of attendants . . . stepping with a pretty and proud gait, like a fawn. . . . Scarce have I in England seen maid so beautiful. She comes putting down each little foot, covered with bead moccasins, light but firm, and smiling out of black eyes." "Angel," "proud," and "fawn" suggest the combination of divine, regal, and natural qualities associated with Pocahontas. Clearly this young woman is a fit consort for the heroic male: "'T was truly a wondrous sight to see this hardy soldier melt, all of a sudden, as the slim form of the girl was there beside him. Her slender shape was like a reed of the river bending in the wind, and her head leaned toward him as the sunflower leaneth to the sun. There were tears in the fawn eyes (I think), but a sudden splendour in the soldier's." The protective male and delicate female meet in an idealized love affair reflecting a southern Eden that envelopes both the people and the land. But not the land as land. In this version, Pocahontas is the land transformed. No savage, the young girl is presented as the European mind would like to see her—angel, virgin, and queen. The English educate Pocahontas and teach her Christianity, seeing her (and indeed the New World) as raw material rather than an individual valuable in herself.

Although Virginia is spoken of as "Earth's only Paradise" when the company of settlers prepare to leave England at the opening of the story, her "river ooze and sultry sun" combine to threaten the European settlement. So trouble exists in paradise, trouble bred by human discontent and natural plagues. Set against these misfortunes is the love of the idealized couple, though subjected to machinations and rumor. When Captain Smith is called home and Pocahontas marries John Rolfe, Todkill assumes that she is faithless but soon finds her weeping for her lost love. The beautiful young fawn dies finally of anguish at the loss of Captain Smith.

But the above description of *My Lady Pokahontas* is somewhat misleading. One further point needs to be made. Cooke's creation of an adoring seventeenth-century narrator who commits himself to a beautiful dream simultaneously separates Cooke from his narrator. And the fact that the dream is from the distant past, a story whose outcome was not only well known but also stressed in Todkill's opening words, underscores conscious awareness of the pastness of the story. A strong sense of artifice pervades the narrative—Shakespeare and the theater are the most obvious examples—and the deliberateness of the artifice is precisely the point to be stressed. Cooke's narrative seems intensely aware both of what is gone and of the tremendous effort needed to create and maintain the myth, be it that of the Pocahontas and John Smith story or that of the antebellum South. The book's importance lies in its existence as an instance of southern enclosure and as a comment on the impossibility of a successfully enclosing dream.

The Yemassee and *My Lady Pokahontas* are manifestations of the southern desire to preserve an Edenic relationship between land and people. The effort to transform wilderness is both the subject and the cause of these narratives. Though the southerner's desire to preserve and the northerner's to expand distinguish them, in both cases the writers of America's accepted canon see preservation or expansion in terms of the possibilities and limits of enclosure. Wilderness is both exciting and threatening to the mind preoccupied with civilization's traditional values. As a result of that preoccupation, some of America's most dynamic writing results when wilderness breaks through enclosure or when the two forces of wilderness and enclosure exist in tension.

William Bradford's *Of Plymouth Plantation* is particularly interesting in this regard, for the story narrates the failure of words to organize or to enclose experience. Commentators frequently note that *Of Plymouth Plantation*'s two parts have significantly different structures. Part 1 typifies the form of the providential history, a story of struggle and success that evidences man's dependency upon God. Because the story of man's redemption and salvation by God was the most complete of stories, the individual or group included in that story would find narrative coherence in the events of life. When Bradford wrote the first part of his history, he was clearly convinced that Plymouth was part of an action shaped by God's hand. The narrative has chapters (evidence of sequential continuity), cause and effect, and conclusion. Human struggles exist within an overarching plan, and thus Plymouth comes into being.

Fifteen years after writing part 1, Bradford turned to the later history of Plymouth troubled by intervening events. The result is a breakdown of earlier form. *Of Plymouth Plantation*'s second part becomes a chronicle, a listing of major occurrences. Earlier shape is gone and with it the confidence that marks Part 1. Significantly, Part 1 ends when the colonists reach the New World, for Bradford's narrative, like the writings of Columbus, cannot carry the enclosing vision into the physical and human wilderness of America. Though readers familiar with *Of Plymouth Plantation* are usually most comfortable with the recognizable form of the first part, one can argue that the real excitement and importance of the narrative lie in the gap between the two sections, a structural gap that points to the effort and failure to carry an Old World story to New World shores.

When the structure of Puritanism began to creak and groan during the second half of the seventeenth century, individuals like Increase Mather and his son Cotton turned to narrative, evidenced in their famous biographies, to celebrate the mission of the original colonists. They did so by enclosing individual lives within a biblical framework. Similarly, Thomas Prince, like Bradford, sought to tell a Puritan story of God's settlement in the New World but found that he could not carry the story beyond the arrival in America. Though eighteenth-century writers Benjamin Franklin and St. Jean de Crèvecoeur tell a more secular story, their narratives encounter similar problems, breaking down before experience. Franklin's vision of possibility for the young man in the New World, for example, cannot be carried through the Revolutionary War. Like Bradford, he is increasingly reduced to recording data and chronologically listing events.

Readers of Franklin's *Autobiography* have struggled so long to locate its thematic or structural unity that they are loath to acknowledge that listing rather than story gradually dominates the writing. And when Crèvecoeur's narrator James sets out in *Letters from an American Farmer* to express the dream of the new man in the New World, a dream similar to that of Bradford or Franklin, he finds his visionary efforts wrecked on the rocks of wilderness and war. His narrative remains a collection of letters (important, as Thomas Philbrick has demonstrated, for their sequential quality) because he cannot enclose the dream within experience.

The existence of imaginative literature within a culture signifies that all of that culture's cards are not on the table; they may, in fact, be nowhere in sight. The desire to get them on the table, under control and neatly arranged, prompts the telling and retelling of tales. It is the very function of the imagination to wonder and question; the culture in which there are no conflicts need not wonder. By telling, literature is also asking. Through written dramatization, an act of communication, other members of the culture are invited to participate in the attempt to resolve conflicts. Literature, then, is something very much like a cry for help; the worse the conflicts, the more they are repeated in tale after tale.

Over and over in nineteenth-century American fiction is the need to tell: the narrator's burning desire to write in Charlotte Gilman's *The Yellow Wallpaper* and the equally ardent desire of her husband to prevent her from doing so epitomize the major conflict—and the paradox—so recurrent in this body of literature. John, as a representative and practicing member of the patriarchy, will not allow his unnamed wife to question her position as a participant in the ideology. This situation at once defines the ideology as a source of the conflict and identifies communication as a possible means to its resolution, a way to alleviate the friction caused by the inconsistencies of the ideology. The narrator's attempt to extricate herself from her position through writing, through language, threatens the opposition; her husband's censorship is the acknowledgment of the power of communication, testimony to the efficacy of telling tales. And no one should fear an oppositional language more than those who stand to lose from it. John *is* the enclosure, and he has become so by the same means his wife employs to save herself: language, because ideology, as a shared construct based upon collective assumptions, exists through language.

The desire to tell, more particularly to find out if experience will work within the framework of traditional structures, is a recurrent theme in the canonical body of fiction. The narrator of Nathaniel Hawthorne's *Scarlet Letter* finds a piece of old cloth and some ancient papers, and he cannot leave them alone—he simply has to tell their story, he has to try and get at their truth. In contrast, Clara Wieland, the narrator of Charles Brockden Brown's *Wieland*, has to tell in the effort to hold back experience and assert her own truth. Like those of Bradford, Franklin, and Crèvecoeur, Brown's narrative has usually been criticized for the very reasons it should be most appreciated—the discontinuities that evidence the narrative struggle at the novel's center. Clara tells us that she writes in compliance with a request for information on the circumstances of her brother's death. She intends quite specifically to honor her brother and to denounce the individual thought responsible for his death; narration is intended to shape and control experience. But a second force actively contradicts her intention, disrupts the structured argument of her narration, and requires that she repeatedly set aside her pen and gather strength for another assault on experience. Similar to though far more pronounced than Mary Rowlandson's in her captivity narrative, Clara's fascination with the excitement of wilderness struggles with her desire for captivity.[15]

What Clara Wieland resists, the narrators in the writings of Edgar Allan Poe embrace; the structures she clings to become coffins in their tellings; and the water she dreads gains prominence in imaginations that welcome fluidity. But the very enclosures they react against provide a stability they discover they have lost. To work within those enclosures denies the experience; to find new forms that will validate their vision and communicate their experience is finally beyond their skills, the dilemma of old language in a new world.

A similar dilemma is confronted by Henry Adams at the beginning of the next century. *The Education of Henry Adams*, poised at the juncture of the nineteenth and twentieth centuries, embodies one of the great struggles between a mind committed to the possibilities inherent within enclosure and the new cultural context of the twentieth century into which that mind is being swept. "What had happened," as R. P.

Blackmur describes it, "was that man had been put in possession of vast stores of new energy which as he learned to use them carried him away. . . . By the end of the century the ordinary man's knowledge amounted to a kind of detailed helplessness before enormous aggregates of supersensual energy. It was a new form of the oldest helplessness in the world—helplessness in the dark."[16] In Jamesian terms, the world had begun disclosing at such a rapid rate that society could no longer rely on its defining enclosures. Adams's effort was to rediscover value, what Blackmur characterizes as a "Center," which would give meaning to the disclosures. "Autobiography for Henry Adams is, then, a scientific fiction which seeks a delicate balance between human ego and ungovernable forces."[17] At mid-nineteenth century, Hawthorne could assume the existence of social centers and focus his attention on exploration; fifty years later, Adams found that exploration negated such assumptions. His autobiographical act, looking back in order to discover patterns, would in itself become the only dependable structure.

The desire to economize force, to consume and transform forces acting upon him in order to thrust himself into his new world, is the drive that powers Adams's imagination. But that desire, that story, is told in language and syntax that betray a distrust of freedom. The narrator wishes to analyze (take apart) what he sees, hoping that when he finishes he may find "life." This faith in the power of analysis is also evident in his story, which is constructed to focus on the periods of intellectual significance and thereby to omit some twenty years of living. The intellectual bias evident in the story's structure is also apparent in the narrator's preference for the periodic sentence. "The manikin, therefore, has the same value as any other geometrical figure of three or more dimensions, which is used for the study of relation. For that purpose it cannot be spared; it is the only measure of motion, of proportion, of human condition; it must have the air of reality; must be taken for real; must be treated as though it had life" (Preface)—the parts of his sentences are carefully balanced to give weight and call attention to those individual parts and to build a mass that, like Russia or the feminine mind (Adams's examples), is not easily diverted from the inertia of its course. The desire for a "leading forth" (an *e-ducere*, an education) is present but overshadowed by the conviction that reason is the best bulwark against inundation by multiplicity. Such an individual is excited by his world but preoccupied by enclosure, the effort "to triangulate the future."

As the body of canonical literature embodies the desire to communicate, it also reveals the stimulus of this desire: to escape from the confines of an inconsistent ideology. Hester Prynne, for example, comes to a new land with a band of individuals who wish to escape from confinement. When Hester does in fact transgress confinement in her affair with Dimmesdale, she is imprisoned, literally and figuratively, by the band itself. Because of her own participation in the ideology of the band, Hester is a willing prisoner: " 'Nevertheless,' said the mother calmly, though growing more pale, 'this badge hath taught me—it daily teaches me—it is teaching me at this moment—lessons whereof my child may be the wiser and the better, albeit they can profit nothing to myself.' " The dictates of ideology, in other words, are so pervasive that even the victims of its assumptions willingly accept them; they do not know how else to think. Hester's remark concedes to the social consensus that damns her, as if she recognizes that there is nothing beyond one's ideology, and anything is better than nothing.

The extent to which individuals may be paralyzed by the paradox of trying to escape from language through language is underscored by Melville's Ahab, one individual who refuses to participate in a system of shared language. Ahab's attempt to escape from culture into an isolated world in which he can gratify his obsession renders him so removed from the shared assumptions of others that his sanity is threatened. The only means of escape for Ahab is by resisting communication, because language is ideology, and he must be apart from ideology in order to accomplish his goal. Toward the end of the voyage, Ahab bids little Pip to leave his side: " 'Lad, lad, I tell thee thou must not follow Ahab now. The hour is coming when Ahab would not scare thee from him, yet would not have thee by him. There is that in thee, poor lad, which I feel too curing to my malady. Like cures like; and for this hunt, my malady becomes my most desired health.' " That which is too "curing" in Pip is the fact that Ahab can communicate with him. Communication threatens his obsession because it might draft him out of his insanity and back into the shared culture.

If Ahab must resist communication to carry out an obsession that runs counter to the codes of his society, he is testifying to the belief that the exchange of discourse has the ability to change the individual. Again we see the paradox of nineteenth-century American fiction: how does one see beyond one's own assumptions, which are shared and reinforced by language, when one is trying through language to resolve the conflicts those assumptions cause?

In the twentieth century, William Faulkner, the quintessential southerner troubled by the physical and intellectual incursions of the modern world, is as preoccupied as James or Adams with language enclosure. Like most southern imaginations, Faulkner's struggles with the implications of bringing Edenic structure into the modern world. Two aspects of *The Sound and the Fury* are especially significant in understanding the author's imagination: its divided structure and the absence of a Caddy Compson section.

I suggested earlier that such works as *Of Plymouth Plantation*, *Letters from an American Farmer*, and *Wieland* provide structural evidence of what happens when an imagination assuming wholeness encounters conflicting experience: the clearly defined unit breaks down. Something very similar happens over and over in the writing of William Faulkner as he probes the implications of an enclosing Edenic myth in a world that no longer has use for it. Like the seventeenth-century story of God's army in the New World, the structure of the Edenic myth is fixed; change has no part in its story. The experience of Bradford indicates that the effort to impose frozen structures on a changing environment leads only to shattered forms. Something similar happens throughout Faulkner, and the crucial word here is *throughout*. In work after work, divided structures repeat themselves, indicating a narrative effort unable to discover a suitable form for the new story.

The absence of a Caddy section reinforces that same inability. *The Sound and the Fury* is presented in sections told by three of the four children of the Compson family and the narrator. When asked during an interview why Caddy was absent as a narrative voice, Faulkner replied that he found Caddy too beautiful to tell her own story:

> [*The Sound and the Fury*] began with the picture of the little girl's muddy drawers, climbing that tree to look in the parlor window with her brothers that didn't have the courage to climb the tree waiting to see what she saw. And I tried first to tell it with one brother, and that wasn't enough. That was Section One. I tried with another brother, and that wasn't enough. That was Section

Two. I tried the third brother, because Caddy was still to me too beautiful and too moving to reduce her to telling what was going on, that it would be more passionate to see her through somebody else's eyes, I thought. And that failed and I tried myself—the fourth section—to tell what happened, and I still failed.[18]

This often-quoted remark indicates Faulkner's reach for something exquisitely beautiful and his awareness of the inexpressibility of that beauty. His statement complements his continuing reliance on the divided narrative, for both evidence the failure of a frozen world in a changing environment, the failure to grasp the beauty embodied in Caddy. Like her brothers, Caddy's creator cannot allow her—or the Edenic world they want her to mirror—the freedom to mature.

Throughout Faulkner, the beauty of the southern Eden fails to find a form to express its unity. When we look for that story, we are handed pieces that we, like the narrators, struggle to reunite. The only daughter among the four children, and therefore the only one capable of giving birth to new life, Caddy "is too beautiful to tell her own story." Kept at a distance, we see Caddy only through the eyes of her brothers, who are themselves fixtures of the shattered dream. We are left with need, division, and loss, longing for that which is perceived as "too beautiful and too moving" to be "reduced" to narrative. Faulkner cannot resolve the issues he so thoroughly defines, as though the burden of the southern myth were too heavy to escape.

In another interview, Faulkner commented that "like anything else, to be alive it must be in motion too. If it becomes fixed then it's dead."[19] We set up, therefore, an interesting conflict in Faulkner's work regarding the southern myth. On the one hand is this consciousness of the need to maintain motion, on the other, this need's functioning within narratives of division in which motion is continually halted. The effort to maintain motion via a form that works against motion succinctly describes the southerner's struggle to understand his place in history. Instead of finding new forms within which to work, Faulkner continued to struggle with divided narrative. Not surprisingly, therefore, for Faulkner, movement in the twentieth century, embodied in such individuals as Flem Snopes and Jason Compson, always comes at the expense of something valuable—sometimes a landscape, often a religious belief, always a way of life. Consequently,

Faulkner's fascination with motion could only express itself in terms of struggle with admired stasis.

The southern Faulkner is usually presented as working with a story distinctly different from that of the North. But the prominence of enclosure in both stories indicates that much more unites than separates these two regions. Distinctions are of course important to make, but my concern has been to underscore the common denominator of enclosure that runs throughout the traditional canon. Over and over, American narrators are torn between their desire to trust the language that defines the new world as an Eden or a City on a Hill and their recognition that the enclosures of culture and language conflict with the experience of life in America. Perhaps it is only the lie of language that gives us a *New* England, *New* Canaan, or *New* York.

In a very real sense, of course, enclosure is a given in any act of artifice. The selecting and organizing of material into a unified whole encloses space and experience. But there is a difference between enclosing in order to embrace and enclosing in order to wall out. When John Winthrop distinguished between natural and civil liberty, his concern was to struggle against the wilderness of natural instincts; disregarding the stultifying characteristics that had developed in the centuries of European tradition, Henry James saw American potential developing only within a similar framework of established structures; and the American southerner could see few alternatives to chaos in the necessary collapse of an Edenic heritage. Traditional American writing, in other words, does not really value a "new" response to space in spite of claims to a "New" world. It seeks, rather, a new *Adam*, New *England*, or New *York*. We might even be accused of being a country that packages new wine in old wineskins.

That packaging has produced magnificent work, much of it made impressive by the tension between old and new. But America has also produced imaginations interested in accepting rather than enclosing and reshaping the potential offered by space; Frank Lloyd Wright, for example, turned from architectural boxes rising above the earth to the interrelationships between enclosure and space. And while European postimpressionists stripped away and took apart surfaces in order to work with underlying structures, the American Georgia O'Keeffe put together the forms and colors expressed in the space of the American Southwest.

Most pioneers in this country tried to transport not only physical connections but also ideas and values belonging to the world being left behind. To the extent that it was possible to enclose the great spaces they settled, these people did so; some cabins were even built without windows to prevent their inhabitants' having to gaze upon the new land. The trading or trapping frontiersmen were motivated less by curiosity about what lay beyond the mountains than by the profits the new lands promised. And the numbers of buffalo, antelope, and beaver destroyed in order for western resources to satisfy eastern expectations continue to stagger our imaginations. Nor does this begin to consider the devastation wrought by mining.

But land and space eventually altered the values of those who settled in the West; the land could be destroyed but not tamed, and individuals as well as families became enormously dependent upon each other and the characteristics of the physical environment. Enclosure could be attempted, but it would not work as it had in the East. I have been discussing traditional American prose in order to demonstrate the possibilities of enclosure explored by the eastern imagination. I want to turn now to other pieces of American prose, works that grow out of a very different response to space, out of the desire to see what happens when the individual explores interrelationships with the land. The traditional imagination, it seems to me, has led to a modern society characterized by disjunction and alienation; I will suggest, in contrast, through the close reading of several central western writers, that there is another narrative working in America, one that offers a much needed balance to the assumptions of enclosure.

2

The Demands of Space:
The Westering Imagination

Emerging from the mud-hole where we last took leave of the reader, we
pursued our way for some time along the narrow track, in the checkered
sunshine and shadow of the woods, till at length, issuing forth into the
broad light, we left behind us the farthest outskirts of that great forest, that
once spread unbroken from the western plains to the shore of the Atlantic.
Looking over an intervening belt of shrubbery, we saw the green, ocean-like
expanse of prairie, stretching swell over swell to the horizon.

Parkman, *The Oregon Trail*[1]

The big sky of the American West has the striking effect of focusing
attention on land as well as sky. In the East, vision is hemmed in; frequently, it must struggle for a glimpse of blue. Skyscrapers, branches
of oak and maple, and the yellow arches of fast-food franchises establish a foreground above which the eye seeks an opening. But on
America's Great Plains or High Desert, the sky so dominates that the
eye is forced toward the horizon, generating a remarkable sense of
balance between the surfaces of land and sky.

There has developed in the West, therefore, an attitude toward physical surface unfamilar to the easterner. In the East, the white male intellect perceives land as needing to be dominated, bent to human will.
Appropriately, it became commonplace among students trained in
New Criticism to dive for "meaning" beneath the surface. And postmodern criticism, while it rejects such diving and argues for awareness of surfaces, does so within a framework that stresses the artificiality of surfaces. Essential meaning does not exist in postmodernism,
but then neither does essential substance.

In the twentieth century, easterners have grown used to idiosyncratic narrative styles reflecting the disjunction of lives in the modern

and postmodern worlds. Again and again tormented psyches wrestle with the grim (and grinning) reality of "mere" surface. One could, of course, emphasize the disjunction by calling attention to the J. Alfred Prufrocks and Quentin Compsons (and Sylvia Plaths) of this century, but an interesting and less frequently cited variation of deceiving surface exists in a 1946 movie widely popular with holiday audiences. Each Christmas Frank Capra's *It's a Wonderful Life* is televised to the enjoyment of audiences apparently never sensitive to the fact that the movie plays frighteningly with surface.

George Bailey's life is "wonderful" because a guardian angel has been directed by a paternal God to save the life George wants to throw away. Without such a *deus ex machina*, as the movie demonstrates, sin and cruelty would be in control. When the floor of the high-school basketball court slides open, throwing George and Mary into a swimming pool underneath, the movie images a world in which surface is both treacherous and fragile (George's brother has already fallen through the winter ice in a sledding accident that threatens both himself and George). In spite of what Christmas audiences want to believe, in other words, their eyes evidence that the world is one of disturbing surfaces protected only by a kindly father—this movie shows nothing intrinsically wonderful about the world in which George and Mary live. Take away George, and people fall upon each other like wolves.

The imagination of the American West, in contrast to the stances of both New Criticism and postmodernism, finds essential value in surface because surface is at the heart of the western experience. Not surprisingly, traditional students, trained to distrust surface, frequently regard western writing as naive. But the western eye regards surfaces as neither hollow nor artificial. Distant from eastern structures and challenged by the big sky, the westerner finds himself accepting the landscape and indeed embracing it for physical and spiritual sustenance. Even the most imposing of surfaces—the landscapes of eastern Utah or the Dakota badlands—seem to share a vulnerability with man while at the same time offering a *visible* stability impervious to the temporality of his threescore and ten.

No wonder, then, that the Anasazi Indians found shelter in such seemingly inhospitable places as the Grand Canyon or the rocky cliffs of Mesa Verde. Man shared a pulse with the earth, and both were subject to the apparent whims of the sky. The kiva, the religious or social center of the tribal experience, burrowed into the earth, the womb for both individual and group. And nomadic tribes could depend upon the buffalo and the reliability of nature's patterns. Land was not a spot upon which to camp but the world within which mankind lived. When whites destroyed the buffalo and drove the Indian from his land, they did more than force a people to shift domiciles; they attacked the very core of life.

White settlers did not share Indian perceptions; initially, they sought to leap the grim surfaces for the more familiar landscapes of the Pacific Coast. But when pioneers did establish footholds in the west, they, too, found physical surfaces a reality with which they had to deal. Response to surface has long troubled the human imagination, for it is much easier to deny and look beyond (or beneath) surface in an intellectual search for absolutes and ultimates—this is the argument set forth by Alfred North Whitehead in his discussion of "misplaced concreteness."[2] Rejection of surface leads inevitably to rejection of individuals and environment—the most obvious instances of such rejection would be the destruction of lives and land in the name of religion or patriotism. In contrast, the fact that western experience necessitates a valuing of surface and discovery of what Harold Simonson calls "place" indicates the importance of a western story as part of the larger cultural framework of America.[3]

The writings of Mark Twain offer a good example of the problems generated by our culture's not knowing how to value surface. In *Roughing It* (1872), Twain discovered that his western experience tested traditionally held assumptions. The comfortable humor in the book develops from undercutting relatively innocent beliefs regarding anticipated danger or excitement—desperados, for example, who do not appear desperate; rocks which only appear to be gold. But Twain's insight moves him rapidly from discrepancies between anticipation and reality to more troubling thoughts on the discrepancies between dream and reality. An encounter with Digger Indians (the Goshoots) leads Twain to question the Indian created by Fenimore Cooper:

> The disgust which the Goshoots gave me, a disciple of Cooper
> and a worshipper of the Red Man—even of the scholarly savages
> in the "Last of the Mohicans" . . . I say that the nausea which
> the Goshoots gave me, an Indian worshipper, set me to examin-
> ing authorities, to see if perchance I had been over-estimating
> the Red Man while viewing him through the mellow moonshine
> of romance. The revelations that came were disenchanting. It
> was curious to see how quickly the paint and tinsel fell away
> from him and left him treacherous, filthy and repulsive—and
> how quickly the evidences accumulated that wherever one finds
> an Indian tribe he has only found Goshoots more or less modi-
> fied by circumstances and surroundings—but Goshoots, after
> all.

Comments on the Cooper Indian are funny, as readers of "Fenimore
Cooper's Literary Offenses" have long appreciated, but the Cooper
Indian is tied directly to the myth of the Noble Savage, of the New
World as Eden, of the white sojourner as bearer of Manifest Destiny.
The challenge to Cooper, therefore, becomes equally a challenge to
America's perception of itself; the piece on "Fenimore Cooper's Liter-
ary Offenses" reaches beyond any particular structural dimensions of
the Hutter Ark to the possibility that nobility and freedom may also be
little more than literary creations.

Twain's insistence that the public see him as humorist rather than
thinker and his increasing bitterness could have developed naturally
from his reflections on the early western experience, for he found it
increasingly difficult to maintain the illusion that discrepancy was
simply funny. The late nineteenth-century "Acres-of-Diamonds" mentality broke down in a world where young men who did go west found
themselves cheated, diseased, and disillusioned. The West tested
myths central to America, myths of individual freedom and romantic
nobility, against a rough and unforgiving surface.

When Twain found his dreams challenged, the surface world
seemed only cold and human beings only dishonest. The problem,
then, in dealing with a story of surfaces is that not only can surfaces
deny dreams, they also seem to leave the individual with few alternatives but endless struggle and bitter memories. Fool's gold establishes
itself as the symbol of a world in which there are no insiders gulling
outsiders. The very fact that an individual has gone west indicates

that he himself has already been gulled by a federal government and a national mythology.

As he presents himself in the opening to *Roughing It*, the young narrator carries with him on the trip out from St. Joseph a large, heavy dictionary. Hamlin Hill has noted that the dictionary is more hindrance than help because old words will not function in a new land.[4] As with the Bible in *The Adventures of Huckleberry Finn* weighing heavily on the chest of the dying Boggs, the impediments of cultural language and beliefs need to be lifted. That burdensome dictionary is part of a struggle in western writing for new language and new story.

Travelers today moving west along Interstates 70 and 80 share Francis Parkman's experience of the opening prairie quoted at the beginning of this chapter. Easterners used to the tall, enclosing pines, oaks, and maples that stretch from Maine to Florida have accepted their world's vertical orientation; they look up to see the sky and appreciate "horizon" only when looking east across the Atlantic. John Smith and William Bradford, two of the earliest Europeans to record what they saw and experienced on America's East Coast, communicate confined, beleaguered existences in which the tiny settlements were overwhelmed more by geography than by natives. The opening of Conrad Richter's *The Trees* describes a moment of confrontation between Forest and Pioneer: "Then she saw that what they looked down on was a dark, illimitable expanse of wilderness. It was a sea of solid treetops broken only by some gash where deep beneath the foliage an unknown stream made its way. As far as the eye could reach, this lonely forest sea rolled on and on till its faint blue billows broke against an incredibly distant horizon. . . . It seemed strange the next few days when Sayward recollected the vision and realized that now they were down under that ocean of leaves."[5] Given such a world, it is not surprising that the eastern imagination works within forests—establishing such protagonists as Goodman Brown and Ike McCaslin and a vertical tension between mind and body, between the sky "up there" and the engulfing land.[6]

To this traditional imagination, used to, impressed by, and comfortable with the struggle against confinement, the disappearance of the forest shocks on many levels, most importantly on the imaginative. Quite suddenly, the eye begins to sweep across great distances, horizon is now all encompassing, and objects far away appear close. The perceiver discovers a horizontal world and consequently must develop a new orientation to the land. An enclosed environment implies escape, for the walls of the forest are close enough to imagine flight. But on the prairie, walls cease to exist; escape seems impossible.

In the East, with the eye confined, the rational powers seek ways of isolating and protecting the individual. But as the western experience strips away enclosure, it discloses a visual world in which the eye is forced into action. In the writings of William Bradford, Mary Rowlandson, and Charles Brockden Brown, the imagination challenges wilderness by imagining control or conversion of it. In the West, the eye is confronted with such space that the idea of domination becomes illusory. Not surprisingly, therefore, the earliest pioneers leapt across this space, seeking Oregon or California, a world physically more congenial to the eastern mind and cultural patterns.[7]

An alternative to leaping the prairie was to maintain the European pattern of New World settlement—to bring along structures that permitted the illusion of dominance. Consequently, one prominent element in many stories of the West is the effort to establish structure within a wilderness. A prototypic narrative of this endeavor is James Fenimore Cooper's *The Last of the Mohicans*. The text opens with a passage that would be brilliantly comic were its implications not so disturbing:

> It was a feature peculiar to the colonial wars of North America, that the toils and dangers of the wilderness were to be encountered before the adverse hosts could meet. A wide and apparently an impervious boundary of forests severed the possessions of the hostile provinces of France and England. The hardy colonist, and the trained European who fought at his side, frequently expended months in struggling against the rapids of the streams, or in effecting the rugged passes of the mountains, in quest of an opportunity to exhibit their courage in a more martial conflict.

This picture presents grown, civilized men so anxious to kill each other as to be oblivious to the environment in which they find themselves. The environment is simply an impediment:

Emulating the patience and self-denial of the practiced native warriors, they learned to overcome every difficulty; and it would seem that, in time, there was no recess of the woods so dark, nor any secret place so lovely, that it might claim exemption from the inroads of those who had pledged their blood to satiate their vengeance, or to uphold the cold and selfish policy of the distant monarchs of Europe.

Concluding the passage are troubling suggestions of rape, a ravaging of dark recesses and lovely secret places in order that policy be fulfilled or vengeance satiated.[8]

At the center of the forest and the center of the text is Fort William Henry, the structure toward which both British and French forces struggle. The fort embodies all the values of family, stability, and military order held dear by the European mind, values for which the European soldiers willingly slaughter each other and destroy the natural environment. However, as readers of *Mohicans* are aware, the world of these intellectually committed but ethically blind individuals explodes in their faces, destroying their fortified structures and thrusting them into an environment for which they are helplessly unprepared. In the first half of the novel, ideas and plans dominate actions as each group tries to outwit the other, but in the second half plans are ineffective, the characterizing imagery becomes visual and disguises the major motif.

The Last of the Mohicans takes place in the eastern forest and certainly does not qualify as a narrative of the Great Plains, but it is without question a story of the West. Its westernness comes not simply from the fact that the narrative is set in 1757, when western New York State was the West; more important to its westernness is the narrative's pattern, guided by the effort of the eastern, in this case European, mind to impose fixed values, symbolized by the fort, on the physical environment, an effort that proves both impossible and violently destructive.[9] As so many later western stories demonstrate, the individual must eventually leave the structure—either return East or learn to live within the environment.

Forts are not the only structures brought West. Perhaps the most effective protection against an unenclosed world is a mental construct that functions even when the physical fort has been abandoned or destroyed. One of the best instances of this effort is demonstrated in

Francis Parkman's *The Oregon Trail*, an account of Parkman's 1846 trip west to study the Indians. Fresh from Unitarian New England and Harvard Law School, Francis Parkman, the son of a wealthy Boston family, left St. Louis in the spring "on a tour of curiosity and amusement." *The Oregon Trail*, like most other trail narratives, was written after the fact and from notes taken on the trip, so we are free to read the initial commitment to "curiosity and amusement" with ironic detachment. To a certain extent that seems a valid approach, for the narrator comes to appreciate, even love, aspects of the land and its native inhabitants. But the overarching imagination in *The Oregon Trail* linguistically encloses itself from involvement with the physical experience.[10]

Shaped in retrospect, Parkman's narrative is the product of a perceiver who controls the structure of his work from the comfort of distance. Narratively, therefore, regardless of shifts in attitude that occur during the course of travel, the "curiosity and amusement" which initiate the trip control the narrative. Parkman provides both a table of contents and headnotes to each chapter, each of which indicates a controlling intellect that advances a narrative not of exploration but of information. Neither the trip nor the narrative is initiated by the urge to discover. Thus the literal center of the twenty-eight chapter text describes precisely what it should—the narrator's life with Ogillallah Indians, because "the journey which the following narrative describes was undertaken on the writer's part with a view of studying the manners and character of Indians in their primitive state." Intention controls structure.

Chapter headnotes in *The Oregon Trail* reflect both the control of a perceiver who can pull together and sum up his material and the qualifying vision that views its subject in highly romantic terms. There are exceptions—Dryden and Shakespeare—but most of the notes are taken from writers like Shelley, Bryant, and Byron, summing up the experience through romantic lenses. Chapter 1, for example, begins with romance and distance:

> Away, away from men and towns
> To the silent wilderness.
>
> Shelley.

Last spring, 1846, was a busy season in the city of St. Louis.

These opening lines envision movement from the noises of urban man to the quiet of nature. The hint of romantic disdain toward civilization will be picked up and maintained throughout the narrative. Consequently, when the narrator returns to the United States, he does so not with joy because in essence he never leaves home. Physically he moves westward, but his imagination remains under eastern control as evidenced in the opening sentence—"Last spring, 1846, was a busy season in the city of St. Louis"—which looks both from the outside and back upon an event in the spring of 1846. There is no "I" in this sentence, nor was there any in the brief preface—"The journey which the following narrative describes was undertaken on the writer's part . . ." The "I" will appear eventually but only after the narrative has established a safe framework within which to move. We begin with a cautious imagination; surprise would clearly be unwelcomed and thus probably will not be discovered.

The narrator leaves St. Louis by boat: "The river was now high; but when we descended in the autumn it was fallen very low, and all the secrets of its treacherous shallows were exposed to view." This statement, taken with the romantically oriented headnotes, indicates the narrative's double commitment to the preconditioned vision of the West as a romantic alternative to urban sprawl and simultaneously to the conviction that civilization is superior to the rural alternative.[11] We should therefore expect to find idealizations of the West coexisting with revulsions at its crudity, both of which are responses of a mind secure in its known world and anxious to wander only to the extent that its assumptions are reinforced.

The narrative voice presented in the opening knows what it likes and is going to find. At the same time, the hints of what it does not like are quickly fulfilled: "On the muddy shore stood some thirty or forty dark slavish-looking Spaniards, gazing stupidly out from beneath their broad hats." Nearby is "a tall, strong figure, with a clear blue eye and an open, intelligent face," who "might very well represent that race of restless and intrepid pioneers whose axes and rifles have opened a path from the Alleghanies to the western prairies." Shortly thereafter, the emigrants Parkman accompanies meet a couple of Britishers, an army captain and "an English gentleman" on a "hunting expedition." The British have a "great disinclination" to any connection with the " 'Kentucky fellows.' " When these two wandering Britishers invite Parkman and his friends to join them, the acceptance is immediate: "Feeling no greater partiality for the society of the emigrants than they did, we thought the arrangement an advantageous one." One almost wishes that irony were at work here, that we were being invited into a world similar to Melville's *Typee*, but such is not the case. An imagination as committed to the East as Parkman's is never going to be responsive to the immigrant impulse which sends individuals out into the wilderness: "I have often perplexed myself to divine the various motives that give impulse to this strange migration; but whatever they may be, whether an insane hope of a better condition in life, or a desire of shaking off restraints of law and society, or mere restlessness, certain it is, that multitudes bitterly repent the journey, and after they have reached the land of promise, are happy enough to escape from it." Physically and mentally the narrator distances himself from these "Kentucky fellows." At various points during the narrative, the narrator moves back and forth within this position of distance, a stance that nicely marks his relationship to the physical world he enters. Their "preparation being now complete," the opening chapter closes with their "cart stuck fast" in the mud of the Missouri River.

Parkman's first chapter prepares us for the narrative that follows, and the expectations established are fulfilled. Chapter 2 reiterates the intellectual and distancing impulse which motivated the journey: "I was anxious to pursue some inquiries relative to the character and usages of the remote Indian nations, being already familiar with many of the border tribes." And he clearly is not impressed with those tribes: "They filed past in rapid succession, men, women, and children: some were on horseback, some on foot, but all were alike squalid and wretched." From this sentence we might anticipate that Parkman will decry civilization's corrupting influence, but his next sentence reveals that his real subject of dislike is the Indian himself: "Old squaws, mounted astride of shaggy, meagre little ponies, with perhaps one or two snake-eyed children . . . and girls whose native ugliness not all the charms of glass beads and scarlet cloth could disguise." "Snake-eyed children" and "native ugliness" indicate an ingrained distaste rather than the more socially judgmental "squalid and wretched." The narrator tells us that he wants to ask questions about a particular group of people, but we must suspect from the beginning that he does not like them and wants to remain distant from them. That he may also be concerned with society as a negative influence is a characteristic romantic stance here complicated by the fact that he sees himself as much more comfortable in "the land of gardens" he has left behind.

Parkman's essentially intellectual pull toward the West, qualified by his preference for eastern comforts, further manifests itself in his attitude toward Henry Chatillon, their guide from the prairie who is more at home in the West than in society. Chatillon is quite probably an admirable figure in his own right, but he is less important than the narrator's highly romantic attitude toward him. The narrator would rather place himself within the authority structure of another individual than envision himself leading his own adventure. Like the "tenderfoot" in Owen Wister's *The Virginian*, he ventures into a new world under the care and protection of a figure idealized in terms comfortable to the eastern mind:

> His age was about thirty; he was six feet high, and very power-
> fully and gracefully moulded. The prairies had been his school;
> he could neither read nor write, but he had a natural refinement
> and delicacy of mind, such as is very rarely found even in
> women. His manly face was a perfect mirror of uprightness,
> simplicity, and kindness of heart; he had, moreover, a keen per-
> ception of character, and a tact that would preserve him from
> flagrant error in any society.

It is very hard to see any of the prairie in this "noble and true-hearted friend," an idealized authority figure who will protect the venturing narrator from the "squalid" Indians who surround him. Thus, guided by Chatillon and accompanied by a British army officer and a British gentleman, Parkman sets off into a wilderness prepared for "a wild but tranquillizing scene" and "little rude structures of logs," which make "a picturesque feature in the landscape." At the same time, of course, he prefers to maintain his distance from the squalor: "Unsheathing our knives, we attacked [the biscuit and bacon], disposed of the greater part, and tossed the residue to the Indian."

The little group "jumps off" from Fort Leavenworth heavily encumbered with British luggage, travels in the wrong direction, and once again becomes stuck in mud, but the narrator fails to see the irony.[12] Nor does he see the humor in his own struggle as a tenderfoot to get

his horse to behave; rather, we are impressed with the narrator's reso-
lute stance and Pontiac's obstinacy in wanting to go back home. And
given the environment that the narrator pictures, the reader cannot
help but sympathize with the horse. "Tourists, painters, poets and
novelists, who have seldom penetrated" into " 'the great American
desert,' " he tells us, cannot be prepared for the actual scene. "Let him
be as enthusiastic as he may, he will find enough to damp his ardor.
His wagons will stick in the mud; his horses will break loose; harness
will give way, and axle-trees prove unsound. His bed will be a soft
one, consisting often of black mud," and "a profusion of snakes will
glide away from under his horse's feet, or quietly visit him in his tent
at night; while the pertinacious humming of unnumbered mosquitoes
will banish sleep from his eyelids." Scorching sun, boundless prairie,
tadpoles in the drinking water, drenching thunderstorms, and the waters of the Missouri River receding to reveal threatening debris complete the picture.

Parkman's simultaneous curiosity about and disgust with the new
land can perhaps best be explained by reference to a theory widely
believed during the early nineteenth century. The unilinear theory of
evolution represented the savage as an earlier state of civilized man,
as an individual in whom we see our rather crude beginnings prior to
the beneficial effects of civilization.[13] The viewpoint accounts nicely
for the narrator's being accompanied by such civilized individuals
as two British gentlemen. Thus the narrator views his adventure as
movement between forts—Fort Leavenworth to Fort Laramie—during
which one must stand guard against the threatening, monotonous,
and ugly environment. In contrast to the ever-present "squalid savages" are the civilized British and the socially acceptable Chatillon; in
contrast to the "naked," "dreary" landscape of "uncouth plants, conspicuous among which appeared the reptile-like prickly-pear," "our
New-England climate is mild and equable." All description is dichoto-
mous, and the effect is to strip away the pleasant illusion of "The
West" to reveal the distance civilization has achieved from such crude
beginnings.

Certainly one can point to narrative sequences in which the narrator
responds positively to his experience. His eye for detail in the early
buffalo hunt or the Ogillallah village leads to a respect for the grandeur of the West and for at least certain Indians: "I do not exaggerate

when I say, that only on the prairie and in the Vatican have I seen such faultless models of the human figure." The association with the Vatican, however, indicates that even when impressed with the physical form of the Indian, Parkman regards the Indian as he would a statue. Indian life remains a subject of scorn. Parkman has ventured into the West intellectually but not imaginatively; he retains his privacy at the expense of involvement. He always views the emigrants from a distance and retreats quickly from forced contact. At Fort Laramie, "for some time our tranquillity was undisturbed" before being "invaded" by settlers or Indians: "Dismayed at this invasion, we withdrew in all speed to our chamber, vainly hoping that it might prove an inviolable sanctuary. The emigrants prosecuted their investigations with untiring vigor." Even the humor in this passage works as a distancing device, with the laughter directed outward—"two eyeballs and a visage as black as night looked in upon us"—rather than inward.

From the perspective of intellectual distance, Parkman draws the conclusion that the Indian "never launches forth into speculation and conjecture; his reason moves in its beaten track. His soul is dormant; and no exertions of the missionaries Jesuit or Puritan, of the old world or of the new, have as yet availed to rouse it." "Dormant" and "rouse" reveal the stance of an individual who sees the savage as sleeping, as needing to be awakened so that he might then progress toward a civilized state. In the previous chapter he comments: "These flowers suddenly awakened a train of associations as alien to the rude scene around me as they were themselves; and for the moment my thoughts went back to New England. . . . 'There are good things,' thought I, 'in the savage life, but what can it offer to replace those powerful and ennobling influences that can reach unimpaired over more than three thousand miles of mountains, forests, and deserts?' "

Parkman's days with the Ogillallah Indians only moderately alter his perception of them as savages. He maintains his superior attitude (earlier he describes a young Indian girl whose dress was ornamented "in figures more gay than tasteful"; in the Indian camp he finds women "tolerably good-looking") despite his portrayal of the Indians as people with likes, dislikes, hopes, and problems. As David Levin describes the effect of these chapters, Parkman saw much but did not allow those perceptions to influence his thinking: "Parkman understands the direction of history but not the nature of Indian life. For him that life exists chiefly as danger and charm, as experience and image but not as value."[14] The anticipated battle between Indian tribes whets his curiosity, for example, but he finds terribly frustrating their tendency to put off battle, their "execrating Indian inconstancy": "I was vexed at the possibility that after all I might lose the rare opportunity of seeing the formidable ceremonies of war." They are simply "ungoverned children" rather than individuals who might be killed. His insight into their daily activities does not dissuade him from believing the Indian is a savage: "An arrow shot from a ravine, a stab given in the dark, require no great valor, and are especially suited to the Indian genius."

As with the savage, so with the land: "If a curse had been pronounced upon the land, it could not have worn an aspect of more dreary and forlorn barrenness," recalling to him "the pine-clad mountains of New-England." As his journey leads him south, then east toward the States, and culminates in a hunt for buffalo meat that borders on senseless slaughter, his disgust with the land intensifies. The description in these chapters is some of the best in the book, but toward the land and its inhabitants he feels no less superior than before:

> Sometimes an old bull would step forward, and gaze at me with a grim and stupid countenance; then he would turn and butt his next neighbor; then he would lie down and roll over in the dirt, kicking his hoofs in the air. When satisfied with this amusement, he would jerk his head and shoulders upward, and resting on his forelegs, stare at me in this position, half blinded by his mane, and his face covered with dirt; then up he would spring upon all fours, and shake his dusty sides; turning half round, he would stand with his beard touching the ground, in an attitude of profound abstraction, as if reflecting on his puerile conduct. "You are too ugly to live," thought I; and aiming at the ugliest, I shot three of them in succession.

Leaving the carcasses, he heads back to camp, his party having shot far more buffalo than they could consume.

Parkman's book is wonderfully rich in detail and experience, but permeating both construction and thought is the enclosed stance of an individual who came West in order to reinforce eastern superiority. He comments in Chapter 19 that "With every disposition to do justice to their good qualities, [the white man] must be conscious that an impassable gulf lies between him and his red brethren of the prairie."

Francis Parkman maintains mental structures that allow him to view the West from the safety of self-enclosure. The subject of his book is the West, but it is told by and for the eastern mind, a mind that finds his story, and its reinforcement of the values of "curiosity and amusement," both fascinating and comforting.

Lewis Garrard, younger than Parkman by five years, also traveled west in 1846 and experienced many similar encounters, but he had a noticeably different attitude. As A. B. Guthrie, Jr., compares them, "[Garrard] not only liked the rude and unfettered life of the frontier; he liked his companions. . . . He liked people. Parkman didn't, save precious few. To his judgments he brought the attitudes of mind associated with Boston."[15] In contrast, Garrard, born in 1829 in Cincinnati, brought attitudes of mind from the then western state of Ohio, attitudes of openness and receptivity to the physical environment. Parkman's judgmental response allows the reader to maintain the comfort of intellectual distance, whereas Garrard's narrative, *Wah-to-yah and the Taos Trail*, conveys the experience of a strikingly new world.[16]

The trip of this young man from Ohio is not initiated, as was Parkman's, out of curiosity or the desire to study the natives in their primitive state but because the "glowing pages of Frémont's tour to the Rocky Mountains in 1842–43 were so alluring to my fancy." Garrard is attracted, drawn by the excitement of the West. Parkman in his opening sentences removes himself syntactically from his trip, emphasizing the past and the city of St. Louis; Garrard, in contrast, makes himself the subject of both the sentences and the action: "In offering this little volume to the public, I must, in self-justice, be briefly introduced. . . . In February, 1846, being then in my seventeenth year, I tossed away schoolbooks, and glided down the Mississippi River. . . . Having made all necessary preparations . . . I crammed my purchases, clothes, etc., in my trunk, put it in charge of the porter, and walked to the steamer *Saluda*, bound for Kansas." Garrard as subject is the initiating force in these sentences, and his verbs—"tossed," "crammed," and "walked"—indicate a commitment to activity. He wishes not to study the West—schoolbooks have been "tossed away"—but rather to involve himself in it. Though his adventure took place in the past, his opening construction puts the past in the past ("Having made all nec-

essary preparations . . . I crammed . . . and walked") and jumps forward into a world of novelty and surprise. In the early pages, he even
shifts into present tense ("As we are all collected") and moves back
and forth easily between the two tenses. This fascinated eye establishes the tone for the rest of the narrative.

Garrard's opening chapter, expanding the anticipation set up in the
first few sentences, describes the narrator as a figure of amusement
(sitting, for example, in "sullen silence") and frequently expresses his
judgments of what he sees. The effect is to call attention to the narrator's changing perceptions. Not only does he continue to use such
words as "astonishing," which suggest his fascination, but narratively
he seems excited by the possibility of bringing the sound and feel of
his adventures to the reader. Parkman's book is remarkably quiet; he
stays away from people and the noises they make. But Garrard gives
us the shouts of the drivers, the new language he hears ("*corralled,*"
"*bois de vache,*" and "*boudins*"), and the feel of the weather. A storm
in Parkman is described but not experienced: "Such sharp and inces-
sant flashes of lightning, such stunning and continuous thunder, I
had never known before. The woods were completely obscured by the
diagonal sheets of rain that fell with a heavy roar, and rose in spray
from the ground." In Garrard, the first rain is strikingly uncomfortable:

> On the 16th we encamped on the "Lone Elm," in the midst of a
> hard rain which poured on us the entire day; and, the wagons
> being full of goods and we without tents, a cheerless, chilling,
> soaking, wet night was the consequence. As the water pene-
> trated, successively, my blankets, coat, and shirt, and made its
> way down my back, a cold shudder came over me; in the gray,
> foggy morning a more pitiable set of hungry, shaking wretches
> were never seen. Oh! but it was hard on the poor greenhorns!

Garrard's eye for specifics (oaks, hickory, cottonwoods; the "long,
shaggy, dirt-matted, and tangled locks falling over [the buffalo's] glar-
ing, diabolical eyes, blood streaming from nose and mouth") and the
feel of the country admit the reader into the discovery of the journey
and into the corresponding value of profiting from both adventures
and misadventures. The values of profit and discovery reveal themselves in Garrard's sensitivity to the struggles of the pioneers; his receptivity to experiences, including those in which he appears ridicu-

lous; and even his structuring of the text, which seems to grow not by intention but by event. Stumbling onto a prairie-dog village, for example, leads him to describe the animal, its amusing antics, and the other creatures found in its villages. Garrard concludes his first chapter by describing another discovery, his appetite for roasted buffalo: his "eyes closed with ineffable bliss. Talk of an emperor's table—why, they could imagine nothing half so good!"

Subsequent chapters in *Wah-to-yah* continue this energetic openness. Garrard does not find in the West the romantic serenity that Parkman's headnotes emphasized; instead, Garrard's West is one of "buffalo straining their utmost to elude the sharp fangs of" persecuting wolves, a world of life-and-death struggles and the pleasure of that energy. He imagines that for "the untaught savage, *such* a life must be the acme of happiness; for what more invigorating, enlivening pleasure is there than traversing the grand prairies, admiring the beauties of unkempt, wild, and lovely nature, and chasing the fleet-footed buffalo—to send death-abiding arrows, with the musical twang of the bowstring—then partaking of the choice parts, cooked by themselves, by their own fires."

Garrard moves enthusiastically toward life in an Indian village. Each event is described in a tone of receptive pleasure, as, for example, when he meets one John Smith: "Yes! John Smith! . . . After leaving cities, towns, steamboats, and the civilized world, and traversing the almost boundless plains, here, at the base of the Rocky Mountains, among buffalo, wild Indians, traders, and Spanish mules, have I found a John Smith. And, probably, for fear the name might become extinct, he has named his little half-breed boy John, whom we call Jack, for brevity's sake." He continues to enjoy the restful contentment of nighttime campfires and begins the longest-running joke in the narrative—eating dog—with himself as the object of fun. He finds the Indians hospitable, curious, and considerate. Parkman regarded the Indians as a lower stage on a continuum toward the ideal of civilization; Garrard, in contrast, appears to regard them as a distinctively different culture, interesting and valuable (in other words, offering value) in their own right.

Another point of comparison involves an interest common to both young men: the young women. Parkman found them fundamentally ugly, their dress more "gay than tasteful." But Garrard joys in their appearance. "The young squaws take much care of their dress" and have a "relieved, Diana look," with each "limb . . . encased in a tightly fitting leggin, terminating in a neat moccasin—both handsomely worked with beads." Their bracelets add "much to their attractions," producing altogether "a pleasing and desirable change from the sight of the pinched waists and constrained motions of the women of the States." He hastens to add, as though catching himself, that he is not recommending civilized women dress "*a la Cheyenne*," "a costume forbidden by modesty, the ornaments gaudy and common and altogether unfit for a civilized women to wear; but here, where novelty constitutes the charm," it is a delight. After his positive response to the "pleasing and desirable change" from eastern ways, Garrard's denigration of the ornaments as "gaudy and common" seems aimed at soothing ruffled eastern feathers. Altogether, he delights in the Indian dress, and he similarly responds to the Indian life-style.

"The different-colored horses, the young Indian beaux, the bold, bewildering belles, and the newness of the scene was gratifying in the extreme, to my unaccustomed senses." Garrard begins to flood his narrative with events of Indian life—the way they raise children, the coy playfulness of the young girls, the love of gaming, the noisy encampment, their sense of honor. "These aliens from society, these strangers to the refinements of civilized life, who will tear off a bloody scalp with even grim smiles of satisfaction, are fine fellows, full of fun, and often kind and obliging." As presented by Garrard, the Indians become a people genuinely different from whites rather than savage ancestors. Garrard struggles to comprehend them in white terms, but "no light can be thrown on their origin" by "the inquiring mind." Perhaps, of course, he is simply not inquiring deeply enough, but the picture he conveys is of a world and a people whose surfaces need to be responded to rather than enclosed and placed on a fixed scale leading to civilized refinements.

Subsequent chapters continue to present the Indians as a society whose customs and values grow out of the working together of highly attractive individuals. Garrard participates and in that participation sees himself as humorous; his humor culminates in the dog-feast joke, where he laughs at himself and eats the Indian delicacy with relish. The effect of these chapters—his humor, his eye for the people and their values, and his structuring of event growing out of event—is to convey the Indian world with a tangible immediacy rather than as an object to be scrutinized from a mental or physical distance. Garrard and his companions leave with a sense of regret; equally important, he has so effectively communicated the Indian world that the reader shares in that regret.

But Garrard has more of the West to explore, and he does so with a similar responsiveness. Winter has come, bringing bitter cold, dreary gray skies, scanty supplies, and trailing wolves. The travelers become, like the buffalo earlier, haunted by wolves, and they discover "the dark side of prairie life." His socks wear out, and his moccasins protect only a portion of his leg. With our attention having been directed to such details and to their hunger, we share the excitement when they finally shoot a doe. As a consequence of this receptive attention to details, Garrard makes us accept the physical reality of a world we have never seen. When, therefore, they at last stumble on a white man's trading post, we can understand Garrard's awkwardness at once more being within a white world. Wearing a breechcloth, moccasins, and blanket, he "could do no less than stare at [the trader's] wife and the other appendages of civilization hanging around, in the shape of dresses, etc., but the woman did not compare, in point of symmetry of features, with my faithless 'Smiling Moon.' "

As his narrative continues, Garrard relishes the dialogue of mountain men and the dangers of their world: "Guards were set and continued through the night. What a train of new thought does an affair like this bring! The anxious state of suspense, the strain of the eyes in the endeavor to penetrate the Cimmerian darkness, the dodging behind rocks and tree, and the stealthy crawl of the older Indian fighters combined to work up to a greater tensity our already high-strung feelings." His receptivity to this experience is evident when he draws the conclusion that "this is the acme of life. With fat, sleek mules, plenty of provision and tobacco, the undisturbed possession of our scalps in doubt, we traveled and camped, always on the alert and ready for any emergency." Though Garrard misses the warmth, security, and physical comforts of the States, commenting frequently on their absence, he is so excited by this environment and so willing to commit its detail to his narrative that the States seems worlds away.

"Here, where the mind is stretched to its utmost tension by reason of the continually impending dangers of starvation, thirst, or the wary

Camanche, Arapaho, Digger, or Apache, his perceptive faculties are quickened, his judgment brought into constant use, and his courage daily tested." In this statement Garrard expresses the ultimate value of his adventures. His clothes are worn out; he has lacked food and warmth; he feels awkward in surroundings heretofore comfortable; he ultimately has to do battle with Indians to save his scalp. But his mind has been stretched. Parkman learned much but under such controls that he cannot be described as stretching. Garrard has plunged into language, dialogue, sensation, and event and has recreated his world for us. We too forget the States, except as a distant, pleasant memory, until at last the trip is over.

In fact, one of the most remarkable things about *Wah-to-yah* is the effect of the opening line in the final chapter: "As we approached the States, running water and heavy timber became more frequent." Garrard has so fully drawn us away from the States that we are startled to realize just how far we have been from everything connoted by "the States." Though Francis Parkman ventured into a new land, like Columbus or Bradford or Crèvecoeur or Byrd, he carried the distrust of surface and the tools of enclosure that allowed him to maintain a mental distance from his environment. Lewis Garrard explored the same world but with entirely different values of perception.

Garrard spoke of stretching his mind; my argument in the chapters that follow is that the effort to stretch language, subject, and form characterizes many of the works created by America's western writers. As individuals who value surface, these writers create works that offer a corrective and a balance to postmodern despair. If we mistakenly assume that the traditional canon, as maintained in college reading lists and anthologies from the major eastern publishers, fully describes the American imagination, we miss a significant aspect of our culture.

3

Divided Narrative:
Mary Austin and Sherwood Anderson

Hamlin Garland's nostalgic *Boy Life on the Prairie* is a text of conventional form—sequential chapters describing the world and maturation of young Lincoln Stewart. Garland's best-known work, *Main-Travelled Roads*, concerns itself not with the traditional story of a young person learning to adjust to social strictures but with the beauty and the toil of life in the Midwest, and it does so in a form distinctively different from that of *Boy Life*. Instead of being organized in sequential chapters, the stories of *Main-Travelled Roads* exist as individual units, providing the earliest literary example of one of twentieth-century America's most distinctive formal responses to space. That I must provide my own name for this form—divided narrative—is central to the argument of *New Ground*. I find the power and influence of the traditional canon particularly evident in the fact that this distinctively twentieth-century form has no name—as though the established literati did not know what to do with it or even hoped that it would go away. Most readers simply refer to it as the "*Winesburg, Ohio* form." In the only study of the structure, Forrest Ingram calls it a "short story cycle."[1] I use divided narrative because division both describes the breaks and implies relationships among the stories. It is the coexistence of these impulses—one to reject and the other to assert—that defines the energy of divided narrative.

Use of divided narrative is certainly not unique to Hamlin Garland. It was used by Mary Austin in *The Land of Little Rain*, by Sarah Orne Jewett in *The Country of the Pointed Firs*, by Tom Wolfe in *Kandy-Kolored Tangerine Flake Streamline Baby*, and by William Faulkner in just about everything he wrote. Sherwood Anderson, Ernest Hemingway, Vachel Lindsay, and Wright Morris all have worked with this structure, which is one of the central instances of an imaginative effort to respond openly to space. Divided narrative rejects the impulse to enclose. It represents both the dissolution of previous structures and the impetus to create new forms. The form's physical divisions, its most characteristic element, function as barriers or gaps over which the motivation (the moving force) within the stories seeks to cross. This function does not describe what happens in either a collection of short stories (where there are breaks but no gaps) or a novel (where there are gaps but no breaks).

As a divided narrative, therefore, *Main-Travelled Roads* is not simply a verbal depiction of crushed lives—though students of the literary canon have chosen to read it that way for years.[2] Garland himself spoke of having written the book in "a mood of bitterness," and the section with which most readers are familiar, the frequently anthologized "Under the Lion's Paw," expresses one of the book's darkest moments. But such a reading neglects, among other things, the opening door of the first story, "A Branch-Road," and the strongly upbeat thrust of the last two stories, "God's Ravens" and "A 'Good Fellow's' Wife." My argument is not weakened even if one, quite legitimately, were to respond that the last two stories are later additions to the original text; the movement from "A Branch-Road" to the original conclusion focusing on the Ripleys is not a shift from naïveté to despair. To conclude with the caring, the laughter, and the concern shared by Mr. and Mrs. Ripley underscores strengths hinted at in such earlier stories as "The Return of a Private," strengths that ultimately prevail over the troughs of despair marking these midwestern lives. It is a mistake, in other words, to see Garland's writing as it is conventionally interpreted, as a group of stories about farmers who wish to flee from their grim lives in the endless reaches of midwestern space and to seek refuge in the security of eastern enclosures; instead, the writing seeths with both anger *and* love. *Main-Travelled Roads* certainly begins with the desire to burn away the economic conditions that have wasted lives, but it undertakes that effort in order for the inherent beauty of land and people to have the opportunity to grow. The structure of divided narrative says that such growth needs form, but not the forms previously used to define the world within carefully restricted terms.

My initial discussion of canonical American writing traced the literary ancestry of divided narrative to William Bradford's *Of Plymouth Plantation* and St. Jean de Crèvecoeur's *Letters from an American Farmer*, works that struggle to preserve the structure of traditional unity amid the threatening shoals of an experiential world. Division in those texts results from the conflict between assumed or desired unity and encountered experience that denies unity. Many eighteenth- and nineteenth-century writers worked to limit that denial, but twentieth-century writers have found the American dream or Edenic myth too difficult to reconcile with experience. Thus the structural divisions that asserted themselves rather uncomfortably in Bradford and Crèvecoeur become the norm in Anderson and Faulkner.

But this process of division is not simply a one-sided rejection of former values. When nineteenth-century evolutionary and psychoanalytic thinkers rejected previous organizing concepts, they did so while seeking to establish new ones. Picasso's cubism, for example, initially decried by many as nihilistic, was in fact vitally concerned with discovering new relationships. An age that shed old values was simultaneously an age that sought values adequate to twentieth-century experience. In prose fiction, Mary Austin and Sherwood Anderson were two of the first writers to reject the values, implicit in traditional novel form, of continuity, direction, and completion. That they were both natives of the nation's interior rather than of its coasts is certainly appropriate to the fact that they saw themselves as rejecting confinement and responding to new demands.

A midwesterner who moved as a teenager to southern California, Mary Hunter Austin (1868–1934) spent most of her life in California, New Mexico, and Arizona. *The Land of Little Rain* (1903), her first and perhaps most important book, is still a work well known only in the West. Owen Wister and Zane Grey were Austin's contemporaries, but only Austin provides readers with a central concern for the subject paramount in western experience, the land. In 1923 Austin published *The American Rhythm*, a text that provides a philosophical argument for the structure of the earlier work. In *The American Rhythm*, Austin sought to "reexpress" what she called Amerindian music, music patterned on the rhythms of the land: "Given a new earth to live on, new attacks on the mastery of time and space, . . . a whole new scale of motor impulses is built into the subconscious structure of the individual."[3] The invading European, says Austin, brings with him his pattern, which must interact with or be replaced by the different pattern that arises out of the new land, for verse forms are shaped by topography and the rhythm of food supply.

In Amerindian music Austin sees the clearest example of a pattern distinctly different from the "dried shell of a locust" of derived English culture. She feels that the Amerindian pattern overlaps with that of the archaic Greek rather than that of the invading European, whose ballad, she says, is "a recessive form, resorted to from secondary motives, and only occasionally rising, in the hands of some native genius[,] to the earlier levels of affectiveness." English verse forms, she argues, are not native but are derived from Greek, Roman, and Hebrew models. As a consequence, "they become the instrument of a selected class, the rhythms of privilege." Amerindian forms, in contrast, are not derivative and are not used for conveying information, as European forms are: "The combination of voice and drum in the oldest Amerind usage is *never for any other purpose than that of producing and sustaining collective states*" (secs. 2, 5).

Rejecting the Freudian premise that the sex and hunger urges are the primary factors in self-realization, Austin argues "that the absorbing business of Dawn Man was the realization of himself in relation to the Allness." Power comes, Dawn Man discovered in the process of dance, by the making of rhythmic movements and noises: "The senses are keyed up. That mysterious awareness of his prey, the instant intake and response to the environment, which is traceable to no discoverable sense, but is of the utmost importance to the hunting kind, appreciates. This is a state so satisfying that it invites repetition." Thus man resorted to the dance when he felt helpless or fragmentary, "when he felt dislocated in his universe" (sec. 6).

These folk patterns of the Amerindian were later reinforced by those of succeeding groups of immigrants. "Something also was added by the land." The classic measure taught in schools was always counterbalanced by the native strain. There was room for play in America but not for the rhythms of privilege. Not surprisingly, Austin finds in jazz or Amerindian songs a rhythm closer to the American experience than the rhythms imported from Europe.

Austin thus presents a case for distinctive rhythm patterns in America.[4] Appropriately, *The Land of Little Rain*, published twenty years before her study of American rhythm, works with a different structural pattern from those found in nineteenth-century writings organized chronologically around the life of a single individual. With few guides before her, excepting the journals of the previous century or the puncturing prose of Twain, Austin recognizes that focusing on the life of the land requires new use of language and form. Consequently, Austin's narrative vision crisscrosses the boundaries of previous structures, seeking to describe the land's living features by breaking through inherited verbal confines. Her technique is descriptive and accumulative, allowing details to exercise their own energies: "To understand the fashion of any life, one must know the land it is lived in."[5]

Like the organisms in the natural world, the essays that comprise this narrative interrelate. The expansive opening shifts smoothly to the concluding "poor world-fret of no account" and then to the water trails of the Ceriso, a delicate world of tiny animals who go about their lives while always scanning the skies for birds of prey. The birds become the focus of the third essay, "Scavengers." Similar connections can be made between several of the essays, but delineating logical unities only partly describes the experience of the text.

Even in its title, which calls attention to language and to the act of naming, *The Land of Little Rain* rejects the Anglo-Saxon sense of self as separate from environment and thus anxious to grasp and define what is perceived as distinct and different. Instead of "Desert," we have "The Land of Little Rain." The Anglo-Saxon penchant for definition Austin describes as the "desire for perpetuity," a desire also manifest in the eastern concern with enclosure, with walling in land that has been literally or metaphorically cleared. The individual who sees himself as distinct from the land can then imagine controlling, walling out, or defining what is essentially separate from himself. The eastern imagination thus confronts, struggles with, and seeks to impose itself upon the land. Naming so imposes, and naming a lake or a mountain after oneself is an effort to give permanence to human transience.

The Indian sees the world differently: "I confess to a great liking for the Indian fashion of name-giving: every man known by that phrase which best expresses him to whoso names him. Thus he may be Mighty-Hunter, or Man-Afraid-of-a-Bear, according as he is called by friend or enemy, and Scar-Face to those who knew him by the eye's grasp only." This practice of naming acknowledges a fluid world where identities are relational and communal rather than tied to a single fixed image or verbal sound. The Indian values a world of common involvement.

The title essay of *The Land of Little Rain* therefore rejects the word *desert* and related concepts. "Desert is a loose term to indicate land that supports no man; whether the land can be bitted and broken to that purpose is not proven. Void of life it never is, however dry the air and villainous the soil." *Desert* is a hostile term because it demarcates a piece of ground that defies man's control and implies an area barren of life. But *Land of Little Rain* makes no such statement; it is a term descriptive rather than prescriptive and pejorative, allowing for whatever living processes might flourish under the conditions of little rain. And the life that exists in the land of little rain is communal rather than defensively isolated; the several parts, the living and the dying, interact, producing a world of cyclic blooming.

In Austin's text, therefore, while the essays do interrelate, one altering the focus of another or picking up a detail and expanding it, the narrative's most powerful effect lies in its affective quality, its ability to depict a delicately rich and fertile environment. The world described by Austin is not hostile to man (or to any living organism); man determines his own involvement. "The earth is no wanton to give up all her best to every comer, but keeps a sweet, separate intimacy for each," an intimacy of "we" distinct from the "I-You" relationships described by Annette Kolodny. Austin's is an all-inclusive intimacy; no Pocahontas to be taken by a John Rolfe or John Smith. Scavenger, rodent, juniper, pocket hunter, or alkaline deposit are all equally "involved," in the word's older sense of "turned toward." The expression of that interaction—among units of the environment and among units of the text—is the achievement of *The Land of Little Rain*.

What strikes the reader in the first and titular essay is its descriptive quality. Instead of imposing a statement or a definition upon the land, the narrator begins with and takes visually from the land. It is a reaching for, rather than an assertion of, definition: "There are hills, rounded, blunt, burned, squeezed up out of chaos, chrome and vermilion painted, aspiring to the snowline. Between the hills lie high level-looking plains full of intolerable sun glare, or narrow valleys drowned in a blue haze. The hill surface is streaked with ash drift and black, unweathered lava flows." Details accumulate, beginning to work together as do the plants within the environment: "The desert floras shame us with their cheerful adaptations to the seasonal limitations. Their whole duty is to flower and fruit, and they do it hardly, or with tropical luxuriance, as the rain admits." The values here are adaptability and doing as opposed to what Austin calls "trying." Whatever the conditions, these plants "do." In turn, the Indians, animals, and birds use what the plants or conditions produce.

In *The American Rhythm* Austin works with parallels between Amerindian and ancient Greek relationships to the land. One parallel, which was apparently lost when man separated himself from his environment and became more "civilized," lies in the common perception that the individual exists within a world of organic (if not cosmic) processes. Though they dominate, the processes must, by definition, value each individual unit. *The Land of Little Rain* accordingly pays attention both to discrete individuals and to the processes into which individuals are swept. The simultaneous focus defines both the story and the structure of the text; essays merit attention individually as well as in their relationships to the larger story, itself about interrelationships.

The essay on Jimville discusses lawlessness in terms of these interrelationships. Western writers, particularly the eastern variety, center many of their stories around the topic of lawlessness, depicting the West as a primordial world lacking law and therefore needing civilization's shaping hand. But toward western "Law" the Jimville essay presents a different attitude, one with important implications for imaginations like those of Frank Waters, Harvey Fergusson, Walter Van Tilburg Clark, Leslie Silko, and Sam Peckinpah.

According to the narrator, the miners in Jimville rely on "hunch" rather than intellectual knowledge, associating the former both with desert and with Greek ways:

> Jimville does not know a great deal about the crust of the earth,
> it prefers a "hunch." That is an intimation from the gods. . . .
> Somehow the rawness of the land favors the sense of personal
> relation to the supernatural. There is not much intervention of
> crops, cities, clothes, and manners between you and the orga-
> nizing forces to cut off communication. . . . Western writers

have not sensed it yet; they smack the savor of lawlessness too
much upon their tongues, but you have these to witness it is not
mean-spiritedness. It is pure Greek in that it represents the
courage to sheer off what is not worth while.

"Lawlessness" thus is the indictment of those who contrast the West
with the traditional world of order as defined by human law. For Austin, however, order results from internal rather than external forces.

In these terms, western lawlessness is the product of an imagination unfamiliar with nature's law. Worth becomes the value of being
able to survive and tragedy not a breakdown of order but a necessary consequence of ordered relationships. Passion and death are
equally accepted. Consequently, the scavenger's food is part of nature's economy rather than cause for sentimental sadness: "Young
Shoshones are like young quail," and a seemingly still field is "busy"
with wild plants working to retake the open space. Not surprisingly,
therefore, along the mesa trail is a rhythm common to both animal
and atmosphere: "It is not possible to dissociate the call of the burrow-
ing owl from the late slant light of the mesa."

Though the pocket hunter described in an early essay fits comfort-
ably within this world, the epitome of the individual working within
the environment is the Indian. Given the values the book develops,
values of physical, emotional wholeness with earth's rhythms, it is
the Indian women who are most especially a part of the cycle of life,
death, and rebirth. Seyavi and her newborn son, we are told, "must
have come very near to the bare core of things" during the time her
tribe was decimated by battle with cattlemen. Together with her "woman's wit," this contact with the rhythms of the earth makes possible
her survival and her art, for all Indian women are artists, individuals
whose lives and artifacts are saturated with the common natural environment. To know either her life or her baskets, one must know the
land. As theirs is a life carried on out of doors, the Indians consequently do not share in the whites' prizing of privacy.

The Land of Little Rain begins by describing the land, then the animals and scavengers whose lives depend on intimacy with the laws of
the land. As the text moves toward conclusion, this sense of interrelationships expands to include man—the pocket hunter, the miners
in Jimville, Indians like Seyavi. The final chapters reinforce this movement toward a holistic response to one's world in contrast to what is

called "house habit." House habit is the enclosing desire for privacy, the perception of the world as "other," which, were it to exist in *The Land of Little Rain*, would necessitate locating such distinguishing markers as chapters. Francis Parkman and William Byrd viewed house habit as a refinement upon the savage state, but in Austin's book the habit is regressive. Indian knowledge is a "sort of instinct atrophied by disuse in a complexer civilization." The white man's house of worship has become a place where he goes to pray for rain; he fails to see interrelationships between weather, land, and use. When storms do come, the white man suspects them of having a personal grudge against him; the Indian, on the other hand, regards them as having too many important things to do—"scoop watercourses, manure the pines, twist them to a finer fibre"—to be concerned with attacking man and his houses.

From this holistic perception, even death is a part of process rather than an enemy, so that the "tragedy" of the young sheep whose horns were caught in the crotch of a tree which then grew around them emphasizes the life of both the sheep and the tree. The two were not at war; it is not sheep against tree but the two locked in a continuing life *and* death struggle. This kind of scene—rather than statements about principles—is central to Austin's narrative and interlocks with the baskets of Seyavi or the working storms to convey a world that values interacting life processes. Thus moments within the text and the experience of the text sheer off whatever is not of worth.

The Land of Little Rain concludes with an essay on "The Little Town of the Grape Vines," a town of Mexicans who enjoy life and seem to understand the book's concern with worth. The final statement of the narrative concerns the town's religious sense:

> I like that name which the Spanish speaking people give to the garden of the dead, *Campo Santo*, as if it might be some bed of healing from which blind souls and sinners rise up whole and praising God. Sometimes the speech of simple folk hints at truth the understanding does not reach. I am persuaded only a complex soul can get any good of a plain religion. Your earthborn is a poet and a symbolist. We breed in an environment of asphalt pavements a body of people whose creeds are chiefly restrictions against other people's way of life. . . . Such as these go to church to be edified, but at Las Uvas they go for pure worship and to entreat their God.

"Edified" (from the Latin word meaning "to build or construct") describes the process through which city-bred worshippers seek knowledge within physical enclosures. For these individuals, religious creeds are one more way to build walls, and worth, law, and value thus become defined in the terms of enclosure.

That Austin's 1903 text has never received anything approaching the enthusiastic acceptance of works by Owen Wister, Frederic Remington, and Zane Grey reveals a great deal about the influence of traditional values in America. But it reveals little about the importance of Austin. Picking up on the openness of Lewis Garrard, Austin's work requires readers who can anticipate a story distinctly different from the "eastern." Western writers subsequent to Austin depend and build upon her narrative efforts. *The Land of Little Rain* is the second of America's divided narratives, an expression of southwestern experience with space and surface. Fifteen years later, when Sherwood Anderson reinvented the same form, it was also in response to conditions which could not be contained by former structures.

The divisions of *Winesburg, Ohio* are usually seen as indicative of collapsing traditional values, but it needs to be recognized that the narrative effort in *Winesburg* attempts to leap those divisions in search of new values.[6] By stressing only the rejection of enclosure, most discussions fail to respond to what Anderson calls "the young thing within," the creative and complementary urges of art and sexuality:

> Perfectly still he [the old writer in "The Book of the Grotesque"] lay and his body was old and not of much use any more, but something inside him was altogether young. He was like a pregnant woman, only that the thing inside him was not a baby but a youth. No, it wasn't a youth, it was a woman, young, and wearing a coat of mail like a knight. . . . The thing to get at is what the writer, or the young thing within the writer, was thinking about. . . . The subject would become so big in his mind that he himself would be in danger of becoming a grotesque. He didn't, I suppose, for the same reason that he never published the book. It was the young thing inside him that saved the old man.

The dynamics and unity of *Winesburg, Ohio* grow from this metaphoric pregnancy, this new life trying to be born into a world that seeks to deny it. Though the breaks between the stories threaten any possibility of sustained development, a major narrative effort is being made to get that "young thing" to live.[7]

Winesburg's "grotesques," as the narrator calls them, are people uncomfortable with and unprepared for functioning in an environment of new freedoms and new demands. In "Paper Pills," Doc Reefy casually tosses rolled-up pieces of paper at a friend. That friend is a gardener, and the narrator tells us that "in Doctor Reefy there were the *seeds* of something very fine" (emphasis added). Images of fertility are frequent in "Paper Pills," but the story is finally one of sterility: the seeds are never planted. The last paragraphs even suggest that, though a doctor, Reefy is more a man of death than of life. The tooth-pulling scene in which blood runs down the woman's white dress may initially suggest intercourse and pregnancy, but we are left finally with an abortion as Reefy extracts and discards a dead tooth. The next paragraphs support such implications as "the condition that had brought her [Reefy's future wife] to him passed in an illness." The woman in fact dies after six months of marriage to Reefy, during which time he reads to her from the crumpled bits of paper, the pills that do not restore health and the seeds that do not germinate.

Frustrated in the denial of their inner urgings by the continuing domination of older values, the grotesques come to fear their own feelings. Wash Williams in "Respectability" (which, like "Paper Pills," is a story lush with sexual images) is destroyed by such fear. In his youth, Wash had been the best telegraph operator in the state. An expert, therefore, at impersonal communication, Wash, like Doc Reefy, had used his talented hands to toss out messages from a safe distance. And like the earlier story, Wash's is concerned with seeds and fertility:

> He made for George Willard a picture of his life in the house at Columbus, Ohio, with the young wife. "In the garden back of our house we planted vegetables," he said, "you know, peas and corn and such things. We went to Columbus in early March and as soon as the days became warm I went to work in the garden. With a spade I turned up the black ground while she ran about laughing and pretending to be afraid of the worms I uncovered. Late in April came the planting. In the little paths among the seed beds she stood holding a paper bag in her hand. The bag was filled with seeds. A few at a time she handed me the seeds that I might thrust them into the warm, soft ground."

An attractive image is presented by Wash, but something is wrong with the sexual relationship, for Wash is seeding the land rather than impregnating his wife, a woman who only pretends fear of the uncovered worms. " 'There in the dusk in the spring evening I crawled along the black ground to her feet and groveled before her.' " Wash responds to his wife as to a symbol rather than as to a human being, and evidently he is comfortable in that kind of worshipping relationship. His final explosion when his wife is thrust naked into the room with him indicates how unprepared he is to look at his world face to face. He would rather live with his illusions, continuing to grovel before the values he felt were represented by his wife.

Wash, of course, is not alone among the Winesburg grotesques in his inability to respond to naked flesh and blood. That condition torments even the book's central figure, George Willard. When Helen White and George come together at the book's end, we are apparently meant to see their relationship as leading to healthy maturity: "For some reason they could not have explained they had both got from their silent evening together the thing needed. Man or boy, woman or girl, they had for a moment taken hold of the thing that makes the mature life of men and women in the modern world possible." I certainly do not deny that the moment occurs, for I am arguing that in such a moment "the young thing" grabs hold of life; however, we must remember that only a few paragraphs earlier George thinks of his relationship with Helen in a way that recalls Wash Williams's groveling: "He had reverence for Helen. He wanted to love and to be loved by her, but he did not want at the moment to be confused by her womanhood."[8]

Noting the continuing desire for reverence, even though individuals in Winesburg have been made grotesque by reverence, points to a timidity reflected in the narrative's structural divisions, but that timidity should not negate our recognition of the book's effort to assert new life. The effort is in fact initiated in the opening paragraph of "Hands," the book's first story:

> Upon the half decayed veranda of a small frame house that
> stood near the edge of a ravine near the town of Winesburg,
> Ohio, a fat little old man walked nervously up and down.
> Across a long field that had been seeded for clover but that had
> produced only a dense crop of yellow mustard weeds, he could

> see the public highway along which went the wagon filled with berry pickers returning from the fields. The berry pickers, youths and maidens, laughed and shouted boisterously. A boy clad in a blue shirt leaped from the wagon and attempted to drag after him one of the maidens, who screamed and protested shrilly. The feet of the boy in the road kicked up a cloud of dust that floated across the face of the departing sun. Over the long field came a thin girlish voice. "Oh, you Wing Biddlebaum, comb your hair, it's falling into your eyes," commanded the voice to the man, who was bald and whose nervous little hands fiddled about the bare white forehead as though arranging a mass of tangled locks.

This opening establishes a world of youth and energy; but, most important, that world is buried syntactically within a statement of decay and frustration. Laughing, shouting, kicking, screaming young pickers of ripe fruit are at the center of the paragraph—and at the center of the book, the town, and the grotesques. To get to them, one has to move past either the "decayed veranda" at the beginning of the paragraph or the "nervous little hands" and "tangled locks" at the end. Like many of the grotesques in the first half of the book, Wing responds to his own internal energy, sensing the need for release. He pounds fence posts to relieve his tension, Doc Reefy tosses paper pills, Elizabeth Willard wants her son to break loose, and Louise Trunnion gives her body in the desperate desire to have someone want it. For each, the energy remains trapped inside, as it does in this opening paragraph; but for each, it is undeniably present.

The "young thing" appearing in many of these early stories is often associated with young people, in particular George Willard. "Mother," for example, refers to the young thing within both Elizabeth Willard and her son. As a girl, Elizabeth sought to release the life within her: "On the side streets of the village, in the darkness under the trees, they [her various lovers] took hold of her hand and she thought that something unexpressed in herself came forth and became a part of an unexpressed something in them." She found, though, as Louise Trunnion presumably did after her, that living demanded more than physical coupling. Life has been stifled in Elizabeth, but she now sees it moving in her son: " 'Within him there is a secret something that is striving to grow. It is the thing I let be killed in myself.' "

Young people—Louise Trunnion, David Hardy, Louise Bentley, Seth

Richmond—are all prominent in the early stories, and each is aware of an inner stirring. But most of the early stories describe failure and inability to give birth to new life. Contrasting structurally with this thematic failure is "Tandy," the story of a little girl given a new name by a stranger, which appears almost at the center of the book. Two things are striking about the story's structural position. First, the young thing within has been given tangible form, narratively as well as biologically, for a child, not a particular child so much as the quality of being childlike, is the subject of this central story. Some inner striving has been brought forth where such earlier grotesques as Wing Biddlebaum, Jesse Bentley, and Wash Williams found that it remained locked within. Second, even though the child exists, the narrative timidity qualifies that existence: the child is female (traditionally associated with home and church) and spoken of as the manifestation of God, worthy of being reverenced.

Though "Tandy" suggests that tangible form *can* be given to the young thing within, that possibility becomes the cause of anguish in "The Strength of God," the story that opens the second half of the book. One of the most vivid representations of the tensions involved in emerging as a child of the new world, "The Strength of God" initiates a sequence of stories that focus on the nurturing of the young thing. If one can indeed argue that the child appears at the center of *Winesburg, Ohio*, then it is suggestive and appropriate that new life move in the direction of adulthood. In "The Strength of God," however, the Reverend Curtis Hartman is not a person of such possibility. Hartman's brief vision of a physical world is far more stimulating than he is prepared to accept; to denounce his feelings he must call upon the strength of God. In contrast to the characters in the first half of the book, Hartman undergoes a release of inner excitement but is so frightened by his experience that he must destroy it. Hartman, pastor of the Presbyterian Church of Winesburg for ten years, is neither stimulated by his work nor stimulating to his congregation: "He was not one to arouse keen enthusiasm among the worshippers in his church but on the other hand he made no enemies." All of this changes when he accidentally sees Kate Swift, who embodies that womanhood Wash and George prefer to avoid:

> One Sunday morning in the summer as he sat by his desk in the room with a large Bible opened before him, and the sheets of his

sermon scattered about, the minister was shocked to see, in the upper room of the house next door, a woman lying in her bed and smoking a cigarette while she read a book. Curtis Hartman went on tiptoe to the window and closed it softly. He was horror stricken at the thought of a woman smoking and trembled also to think that his eyes, just raised from the pages of the book of God, had looked upon the bare shoulders and white throat of a woman.

Hartman's previous experience with women had been only the "formal and prolonged courtship" with his wife. He "had never permitted himself to think of other women. What he wanted was to do the work of God quietly and earnestly." But he cannot deny his fascination with "the bare shoulders and white throat of a woman"; he even experiences a mild transformation: "With his brain in a whirl he went down into the pulpit and preached a long sermon without once thinking of his gestures or his voice. The sermon attracted unusual attention because of its power and clearness." The power and clarity are expressions of Hartman's visual contact with bare and white skin, the physical world he has always avoided but to which he is undeniably capable of responding.[9]

Like anyone divided against himself, the pastor struggles to reconcile his contradictory impulses. "He did not want to kiss the shoulders and the throat of Kate Swift and had not allowed his mind to dwell on such thoughts. He did not know what he wanted. 'I am God's child and he must save me from myself,' " cries Hartman, echoing the words of Melville's Father Mapple: "To obey God is to disobey yourself." Hartman's cry is clearly that of an individual who has been trained to distrust the human body. The words reflect the anguish of a late-nineteenth-century man suddenly shown that he does not occupy a place midway between the angels and the animals, that he is in fact one of the animals, a man who when forced to look at his physical world for the first time can only sense the collapse of his sacred absolutes. The struggle in Curtis Hartman is between belief in something beyond humanity and the urge to respond to the excitement of his world:

> "I want to look at the woman and to think of kissing her shoulders and I am going to let myself think what I choose," he declared bitterly and tears came into his eyes. . . . "I shall go to some city and get into business," he declared. "If my nature is such that I cannot resist sin, I shall give myself over to sin. At

least I shall not be a hypocrite, preaching the word of God with
my mind thinking of the shoulders and neck of a woman who
does not belong to me."

Hartman's powerfully divisive drives seem certain to bring him to
self-destruction until the night when he sees "the woman of sin [be-
gin] to pray." At that moment he rushes to George Willard and de-
clares himself saved, for he no longer has to see her as a person. He
can again imagine Kate Swift as "an instrument of God, bearing the
message of truth," a symbol rather than a human being.

The woman who attracts Hartman is the subject of the next story,
"The Teacher."[10] As a physical being who smokes and has traveled
widely, Kate Swift excites the minds of young students such as George
Willard: "He took a pillow into his arms and embraced it thinking first
of the school teacher, who by her words had stirred something within
him." On the particular night of her story, "it was as though the man
and the boy [Hartman and Willard], by thinking of her, had driven
her forth into the wintry streets," her mind "ablaze with thoughts of
George Willard." The energy that sets Kate into motion excites the
young thing within George. This is in many ways a sexual response,
and what is being stimulated is a passion for life: " 'You will have to
know life,' she declared, and her voice trembled with earnestness. . . .
'If you are to become a writer you'll have to stop fooling with words,'
she explained. 'It would be better to give up the notion of writing until
you are better prepared. Now it's time to be living. I don't want to
frighten you, but I would like to make you understand the import of
what you think of attempting. You must not become a mere peddler of
words.' "

The young thing within, the growth of the individual, and the development of the artist finally come together in "The Teacher," reinforcing the suggestions made in the introductory "Book of the Grotesque" and pointing to the one story in *Winesburg, Ohio* that deals
specifically with the life of an artist. That story, "Loneliness," immediately follows "The Teacher." Enoch Robinson had desired to be an artist, but he had failed because "he was always a child and that was a
handicap to his worldly development. He never grew up and of course
he couldn't understand people and he couldn't make people understand him." It is apparently not enough simply to give birth to the
young thing; that child must be allowed to grow and mature if it is to

flourish as a healthy adult. In other words, the presence of "Tandy" is important to the structure of *Winesburg, Ohio*, but childhood is only a step, not the final stance.

"The story of Enoch," the narrator tells us, "is in fact the story of a room almost more than it is the story of a man." This could be said of everyone's story in *Winesburg, Ohio* because all the grotesques live in enclosures that they or others have constructed. Like Wash and Curtis before him, Enoch lives in a box because he is not prepared to look directly at the world of concrete particulars: "The child in him kept bumping against things, against actualities like money and sex and opinions." In contrast to Kate Swift, Enoch turns to art as to a retreat, just as he had when he was a schoolboy and his reading allowed him to remain unaware of his environment: "Drivers of teams had to shout and swear to make him realize where he was so that he would turn out of the beaten track and let them pass." Even when Enoch paints, he manages to avoid particulars. He likes to talk about "the point" of a painting, a point that, appropriately, no one else can see: " 'It's a woman you see, that's what it is! It's a woman and, oh, she is lovely! . . . I didn't try to paint the woman, of course. She is too beautiful to be painted.' " Enoch fails to look at people, so when he marries (because he wants "to touch actual flesh-and-bone people with his hands"), he dooms his marriage to a collapse similar to that in "Respectability." The brief description of his family—"Two children were born to the woman he married"—suggests that he was somehow not physically involved in their conception. Once his marriage ends, he prefers his room, which he peoples with invented shadows. When spoken of, these shadows, unlike the children begotten by his former wife, are directly related to Enoch's creative powers. Enoch lives in a box, and there his art thrives. This world of shadows comes to an end when another woman enters his room: " 'She was too big for the room. . . . She was so grown-up, you see.' " When life intrudes upon the walled-in existence of Enoch, it shatters his illusions and leaves him lonely because all he has known is retreat. Like Curtis Hartman and Wash Williams, Enoch Robinson does not know how to begin looking at his world.

George Willard must avoid this perception of art as a retreat.[11] Anderson suggests that the artist in the twentieth century must not be someone for whom words are little boxes into which abstractions of life can be fitted. He must desire instead to look at such actualities as human skin and to respond to the physical life swelling underneath. After Enoch's story, "Loneliness," comes George's, "Awakening," and in this story words seem to have a new pregnancy for George. "He felt unutterably big and remade by the simple experience through which he had been passing and in a kind of fervor of emotion put up his hands, thrusting them into the darkness above his head and muttering words. The desire to say words overcame him and he said words without meaning, rolling them over on his tongue and saying them because they were brave words, full of meaning. 'Death,' he muttered, 'night, the sea, fear, loveliness.' " George has previously maneuvered these empty boxes on the pages of the Winesburg *Eagle*, but now he senses in the material an excitement that might allow him to tell stories of life rather than death. The physical beatings he takes in "Awakening" and in "Queer" arouse in George the sense of his own pomposity. He must learn the same thing with regard to language in order to use the power of the medium to express and develop the life within.

That life, which will be George's subject, is nowhere more evident than in one of the final scenes, when George prepares for his departure from Winesburg:

> On all sides are ghosts, not of the dead, but of living people.
> Here, during the day just passed, have come the people pouring
> in from the town and the country around. Farmers with their
> wives and children and all the people from the hundreds of little
> frame houses have gathered within these board walls. Young
> girls have laughed and men with beards have talked of the af-
> fairs of their lives. The place has been filled to overflowing with
> life. It has itched and squirmed with life and now it is night and
> the life has all gone away. The silence is almost terrifying. . . .
> One shudders at the thought of the meaninglessness of life
> while at the same instant, and if the people of the town are his
> people, one loves life so intently that tears come into the eyes.

In spite of the frustrations that demand attention in the lives of the grotesques of Winesburg, the town and the people "squirm" with life. The structural divisions of the narrative do indeed isolate individual stories, but the book's narrative urge ultimately leaps across those divisions, grasping the relationships among the stories and the vital impulses within the grotesques to seek out others and to tell their sto-

ries. Indeed, the narrative act of establishing connections is so important in *Winesburg, Ohio* that one of the dominant charcteristics of so
many grotesques is their desire to narrate to George Willard their own
inner squirmings.

For Sherwood Anderson, the impulse to function physically within
the environment correlates with the urge to function verbally. That is
what Kate Swift tells George Willard, and that is why the grotesques
of Winesburg are "impelled" individuals who seek to become "articulate," to give birth to the "young thing within" through the act of
telling their stories. Though their impulsion is frequently thwarted,
George's is not—it drives him forth from Winesburg to seek new life
and perhaps a new story.

4

Hemingway: The Body as Matrix

American writing in the first decade of the twentieth century witnessed the rise of a new geographic area of dominance—the Midwest. During those years many young imaginations were leaving the Winesburgs and were drawn to the energies of Chicago. Shifting population density and better communication certainly accounted for much of the Midwest's prominence; equally important was the Midwest becoming a point of increasing contact between East and West. The midwestern industrial base economically integrated western resources into products that could contribute to eastern commerce. The Midwest for both eastern and western strengths became a point of conversion, of which the steel industry is the most obvious example. The Midwest was inevitably to become a new area of economic power and imaginative possibility.

When one reads midwestern writing—*Winesburg, Ohio, Giants in the Earth, Boy Life on the Prairie, My Ántonia, The Home Place, Old Jules, The Great Gatsby, In Our Time*—one is struck by the overwhelming sense of nostalgia that dominates so much of the work. We do not find that quality in such force anywhere else in American writing. Even in southern writing, which might seem an appropriate comparison, *nostalgia* is not a useful term—at least not until the agrarian movement of the twentieth century. In the nineteenth century, the South found itself working to create and later to preserve an Anglo-Saxon image of Eden. But the Midwest was settled by large numbers of immigrants who looked back to older cultures and values. They could not preserve, however, what no longer existed. As those same immigrants struggled with the place of their dream in their new homeland, the gap between dream and everyday reality increased their sense of loss.

A significant distinction, therefore, emerged between nostalgia of the Midwest and that of the late nineteenth-century New South; the midwestern imagination looked back as a prelude to moving forward. The beauty of the antebellum southern plantation was an expression of the New South's desire to idealize, to fix a lost way of life. But the midwestern imagination does not dwell on loss; it uses contact with the past to initiate activity.

We have already seen in Sherwood Anderson's *Winesburg, Ohio* how divided narrative integrates a consciousness of lost past with an impulse to new unity. But perhaps because Anderson himself was part of an older world (he was born in 1876), he was never able to advance his story. A successor in the midwestern imagination, Ernest Hemingway, also begins with divided narrative but builds on its inherent impulse toward the new.

Relevant to this study and crucial to an understanding of Hemingway's work is emphasis on his midwestern heritage. Born in Oak Park, Illinois, in 1899, Hemingway spent his first eighteen years in Illinois and Michigan.[1] When he went east, he was in transit to the fighting in World War I. His return in 1919 brought him home to Illinois, where he remained until 1921. It is certainly reasonable, therefore, to consider Hemingway as a midwesterner. Emphasizing his background is important because it helps to explain why among eastern academics of the 1970s and 1980s Hemingway's literary star has fallen so sharply. He is attacked by feminists and poststructuralists alike and is seen by many as a voice for the period between the wars, a voice whose greatness has had its day. But I want to stress that Hemingway's imagination is not eastern in order to focus on what I see his work doing. Unlike Faulkner, his contemporary, Hemingway is not preoccupied with enclosure, not primarily concerned with the tension between structure and wilderness. Like other western and midwestern writers, his effort is to move away from that tension. Together with Garland, Sandburg, Cather, Sandoz, Rølvaag, and Anderson, Hemingway remained fascinated with space and the physical environment of which his early years made him a part.

Because so much of the literary canon of the American twentieth century is dominated by the modern sense of loss, critics often catalog Hemingway's work and fit it into the writings of the lost generation.[2] Certainly we can choose to restrict our understandings of Hemingway to *The Sun Also Rises* or a narrow reading of *A Farewell to Arms*, but such restriction does woeful injustice to an imagination that moves toward its most remarkable expression in *Green Hills of Africa*. This imagination begins by rejecting suffocating traditional enclosures and works to see if there are not ways to align individual lives with natural patterns. Given the tendency of academics to focus on the parts of Hemingway that extend the traditional canon, it is not surprising that such a work as *Green Hills of Africa* is not only neglected but actively disliked.[3] To ask about the importance of *Green Hills* to Hemingway and to American literature necessitates restructuring assumptions both about Ernest Hemingway and about a single American literary canon.

Before turning to the divided narrative of *In Our Time* (1924) and to the work that ultimately grows out of it, *Green Hills of Africa* (1935), I want to indicate briefly the result of rethinking our assumptions about Hemingway's work by calling attention to the narrative technique of *A Farewell to Arms* (1929). This novel does not receive the academic attention accorded *The Sun Also Rises* in part because feminist critics have never liked Catherine Barkley and in part because it is not as intensely "lost" as *The Sun Also Rises*. However, loss is not where we should focus our attention. After all the themes and patterns have been traced through *A Farewell to Arms*, the single most important aspect of the book—the fact that the narrative is first person—has frequently not been touched. Hemingway gives us not the events that culminate in the death of Catherine but rather the expression of an imagination that begins to operate after Frederic Henry leaves Catherine's deathbed and walks into the spring rain.

A Farewell to Arms, in other words, is not a story of loss but of the effort to make a beginning. Henry does not reminisce about a lost love but asks how, with his assumptions having been so thoroughly changed, to build on that experience. His answer begins with the expression that is the text of *A Farewell to Arms*. Not about loss or about the love affair of Frederic and Catherine, *A Farewell to Arms* is rather the expression of an individual prepared to make a new beginning. Like so many works of the Midwest, this narrative looks back as part of the process of going forward, and it is the going forward that we lose sight of when we try to fit the book into assumptions about a lost generation. The effort of Frederic Henry in fact prefigures the work of the 1930s, *Death in the Afternoon* and *Green Hills of Africa*.

Green Hills is the story of an individual becoming healthy and therefore seeking to get the most out of himself. The successful integration of self, world, and art defines the achievement of this fine work. The impulse to health that culminates in *Green Hills* is initiated in Hemingway's first book, *In Our Time*, where loss, death, and division define the conditions of Nick Adams's world. Though Nick never solves the problem of unity, as evidenced by the book's fragmented structure, he does initiate a movement toward health, a movement that begins with the physical.[4] In the western or midwestern imagination, one must begin with the physical because the body is seen not as a corpus, a container for an essential spirit, but as a locus, the matrix of life.

The physical world screams with life in the opening pages of *In Our Time*, screams almost entirely those of pregnant women or women with young children. In the disturbingly quiet environment of *Winesburg, Ohio*, the "young thing within" struggled against the constrictions of old ideas. In Hemingway, that young thing comes kicking and screaming into a violent, bloody world where the first condition is war. The screams of women contrast with the narrative tone in the first story, "On the Quai at Smyrna," which establishes a protective distance for the speaker: "The Greeks were nice chaps too. When they evacuated they had all their baggage animals they couldn't take off with them so they just broke their forelegs and dumped them into the shallow water. All those mules with their forelegs broken pushed over into the shallow water. It was a pleasant business. My word yes a most pleasant business."

"Indian Camp," the story introducing Nick Adams, presents many of the same circumstances but with a response from Nick crucially different from that of the previous speaker. Once again the story turns on the screams of a pregnant woman, but instead of remaining *on the quai*, Nick and his father take a boat into the water and go directly to the woman giving birth. In this early story, Nick is essentially passive, being rowed across the water and resting in his father's arms. He enters the physical world but not on the basis of his own strengths. His initial reaction to the pregnant Indian woman's screams is to look away: " 'Oh, Daddy, can't you give her something to make her stop screaming?' " All the males encountered early in the book wish to stop the screams of life in one way or another—Nick turns away, the Indian woman's husband cuts his throat, and Nick's father hides himself behind a wall of professionalism.

But the father's "post-operative exhilaration" quickly disappears once he looks at the Indian husband's cut throat. In contrast, Nick is filled with questions: " 'Do ladies always have such a hard time having babies . . . Why did he kill himself, Daddy . . . Do many women . . . is dying hard, Daddy?' " Nick has had a good look at both the screaming woman giving birth and the dead Indian and has discovered a fascination that reveals itself in his questions about life and death, men and women.

This divided narrative not only gives us a sequence of stories, as does *Winesburg, Ohio*, but also alternates those stories with a sequence of "interchapters" that puts Nick's world in the context of "In Our Time." In the second interchapter, a Greek cavalry herds a procession of refugees through rain and mud, and another woman is giving birth. The insistent appearance of life in the midst of a dirty and violent physical environment characterizes much of the opening material in the book, where the dual concerns of death and life dominate all other considerations. That duality is one of the distinctive features of the book—structurally, in the division between interchapters and stories, and thematically, in the number of couples who fail to relate to each other verbally or physically. In the midst of this division, the effort of Nick Adams to begin living parallels the struggles of babies to be born.

The interchapters separating the stories of Nick's break with home continue to stress the ugly, violent world of war and to employ distancing understatement in the attitudes expressed and the language used: "It was a frightfully hot day. We'd jammed an absolutely perfect barricade across the bridge. It was simply priceless. . . . It was absolutely topping. They tried to get over it, and we potted them from forty yards. . . . It was an absolutely perfect obstacle. Their officers were very fine. We were frightfully put out when we heard the flank had gone, and we had to fall back." The skill being enjoyed here is not the skill that Nick seeks to develop. Nick will learn to hunt and to fish, but the men in war rear clever impediments that enable them to destroy for the sake of destroying.

Nick's world with his parents and friends has thus far been structurally separated from the violent world characterized in the interchapters, but Nick moves toward confronting the new sphere. The sixth interchapter brings the two worlds together. The previous interchapter had ended with a minister sitting against the wall of a hospital before he is shot. Now Nick is in a similar position against the wall of an equally useless social institution: "Nick sat against the wall of the church where they had dragged him to be clear of machine-gun fire in the street. Both legs stuck out awkwardly. He had been hit in the spine." The book has suddenly integrated the public world of war and the private world of individual growth. As a consequence, the early distictions between Nick's stories and those of the interchapters are not so easily maintained. This is particularly clear in "Soldier's Home" when young Krebs returns from the fighting.

The title of "Soldier's Home" stresses not the soldier but his home, a world Krebs is no longer part of: "Krebs went to the war from a Methodist college in Kansas. There is a picture which shows him among his fraternity brothers, all of them wearing exactly the same height and style collar. . . . There is a picture which shows him on the Rhine with two German girls and another corporal. Krebs and the corporal look too big for their uniforms. The German girls are not beautiful. The Rhine does not show in the picture." The two pictures depict two irreconcilable worlds between which Krebs must choose. The first is that of the conventional, ordered home life of his youth; the second depicts his life overseas and punctures romantic conventions by means of a sharp eye for detail. Ironically, the first world, the clean, neat home life, demands the most emotional complexity:

> Later he felt the need to talk but no one wanted to hear about it. His town had heard too many atrocity stories to be thrilled by actualities. Krebs found that to be listened to at all he had to lie. . . . All of the times that had been able to make him feel cool and clear inside himself when he thought of them; the times so long back when he had done the one thing, the only thing for a man to do, easily and naturally, when he might have done something else, now lost their cool, valuable quality and then were lost themselves.

The war offered Krebs a valuable experience, one in which an individual who had previously dressed and thought precisely like everyone else was forced to discover his own abilities in order to survive in places like the Belleau Wood and the Argonne. But the world at home wants conventions and lies; it wants the boy to put his collar back on.

Krebs's worlds are not just irreconcilable—few would wish to bring the filth and death of war back home—but destructive of each other. As a result of his experience, Krebs sees that the ideals of his society threaten to destroy him and his new values. "Krebs acquired the nausea in regard to experience that is the result of untruth or exaggeration." Sickness rather than health awaits him at home, sickness imaged in the entangling relationships that demand carefully detailed rules and patterns of behavior.

Krebs is not sure what he is going to do, but the values of something clean and simple attract him. Complex patterns deny individual skills except as outlined by the group. Health demands new relationships. What Krebs seeks begins to be realized by Nick Adams in "Cross-Country Snow." After the filth and complications of previous experience, skiing in the clean cold of the mountains offers the potential for experiencing through the senses: "The rush and the sudden swoop as he dropped down a steep undulation in the mountain side plucked Nick's mind out and left him only the wonderful flying, dropping sensation in his body." Nick enjoys something here that had eluded him in "The End of Something" and that eludes Krebs in "Soldier's Home"—he feels good. Complicated relationships are replaced by a clean world of direct physical pleasure and by Nick and his friend George enjoying themselves and each other's company.

Given the atmosphere of healthy activity in this story, it is appropriate that "Cross-Country Snow" be the first story in which pregnant women appear in something other than conditions of war. Nick and his wife are expecting a baby. He may henceforth have to sacrifice some of the good skiing, but that is not something he worries about. The full and pleasurable experience of the moment constitutes a good life, not a retreat from the world but an experiencing of what the world offers.

Sensual values are again in evidence in "Big Two-Hearted River," where Nick also makes some intellectual choices. Nick has cleansed his body and his senses and has developed his physical skills during the course of the book. If he is not to remain an individual limited to the power of his senses, the intellectual and imaginative powers must be developed as well. That integration is not achieved in Hemingway's work until *Green Hills of Africa*, but Nick initiates movement in that direction as he becomes intellectually as well as physically responsive to his environment.

However, the most obvious condition of Nick's world, division, continues to be evident. Like the whole of *In Our Time*, "Big Two-Hearted River" is a divided narrative, two parts that detail an individual's experience on a river whose very name stresses division. For the first time in the book, Nick is alone. No longer relying upon or sharing his experience with someone else, he is fully capable of functioning alone in his environment. "The End of Something" and "Big Two-Hearted River" both open with scenes of urban decay, but whereas before Nick had ended something, now he is beginning.[5]

The first part of "Big Two-Hearted River" emphasizes Nick's outdoor skills—"He did not need to get his map out. He knew where he was from the position of the river"—skills most obvious in his careful attention to physical detail:

> Between two jack pines, the ground was quite level. He took
> the ax out of the pack and chopped out two projecting roots.
> That leveled a piece of ground large enough to sleep on. He
> smoothed out the sandy soil with his hand and pulled all the
> sweet fern bushes by their roots. His hands smelled good from
> the sweet fern. He smoothed the up-rooted earth. He did not
> want anything making lumps under the blankets. When he had
> the ground smooth, he spread his three blankets. One he folded
> double, next to the ground. The other two he spread on top.

Nick knows what he is doing, and that knowledge combined with his new environment produce the pleasure of a "good place to camp" and a "good smell."

Part 2 of "Big Two-Hearted River" shows Nick paying the same scrupulous attention to detail while having to control himself because he is "excited by the early morning and the river." Doing things carefully is in part a way to exercise control, to ensure that they are done well and that he appreciates each aspect of the trip. In this last story, Nick steps into the river and thereby completes an action begun in "Indian Camp." Water has been a central image throughout the book, but this is the first time Nick has entered it. Initially rowed across water while he trailed his hand, Nick has brought himself to the point where he and his physical environment are in direct contact. And, appropriate to the book's concern with a living world, Nick's fishing is described as though he were now intimately involved with life: "Holding the now living rod across the current, he brought in the line with his left hand.

The rod bent in jerks, the trout pumping against the current. . . . There was a long tug. Nick struck and the rod came alive and dangerous . . . Nick swung the rod against the pull. It felt as though he were hooked into the log itself, except for the live feeling." It is not just that the fish is living; the quality of life is coextensive with the pulsating rod and with Nick himself. His emotions have begun to throb, and Nick is careful to savor them as much as the buckwheat pancakes or the onion sandwiches: "Nick climbed out onto the meadow and stood, water running down his trousers and out of his shoes, his shoes squlchy. He went over and sat on the logs. He did not want to rush his sensations any." This is not, as many readers would have it, a sensual indulgence but an intellectual awareness of his senses. Nick is alive to the camp and to the river and to himself.

But there is still the swamp:

> Nick did not want to go in there now. He felt a reaction against deep wading with the water deepening up under his armpits, to hook big trout in places impossible to land them. In the swamp the banks were bare, the big cedars came together overhead, the sun did not come through, except in patches; in the fast deep water, in the half light, the fishing would be tragic. In the swamp fishing was tragic adventure. Nick did not want it. He did not want to go down the stream any further today.

Of course, the swamp, like death and the violence of war, cannot be monastically avoided. The end of *In Our Time* implies that Nick will someday fish the swamp, will wade into the water, and will be capable of functioning there as well as in the clean, cold world of the high ground.

Nick's intellectual distinction between the swamp and the high ground initiates the effort of the Hemingway hero to develop both understanding and physical skills. As the Hemingway story shifts to first-person narrative, the effort is to integrate physical, intellectual, and imaginative skills, an effort occurring as we move from *The Sun Also Rises* to *A Farewell to Arms* and finally to *Green Hills of Africa*. Nick Adams initiates this process by valuing life and by rejecting any techniques in tone or intellectual stance that distances the self from the screams of life. These efforts eventually culminate in *Green Hills of Africa*, and a new imagination asks about the relationship between the patterns of an individual life and those of the physical world. Hemingway's fictionalizing of biography, his integrating art and life, allows him to explore the possibilities inherent in moving from observation of the natural world to interrelationship with it.

In the foreword to *Green Hills of Africa*, the protagonist/narrator tells us that he seeks the "shape and pattern" of a country and a life. He establishes his interest in what life *does* as opposed to what life *is*, as Henry David Thoreau defined the latter in a similar effort. Thoreau went to Walden Pond to study, seemingly avoiding consumption of (taking into himself) the environment. He wanted, he says in *Walden*, to "drive life into a corner." The narrator of *Green Hills*, however, eats the kidneys and liver (the purifying organs) of the kudu, for he seeks not to perceive life from a distance but to become a part of living processes.

As indicated by the title's first word, a word that receives particular stress by the omission of the anticipated definite article, the chief characteristic of the narrator's world is its organic quality. Not "the hills" but "green" is the focus of the title, and the green in the hills of Africa is chlorophyll, a pigment that makes possible photosynthesis, the process of consumption whereby a plant transforms external energy into internal growth. Consumption and transformation are the dominant images in the book and the motivating urges in the narrator himself. Art in general and the act of writing *Green Hills* in particular parallel the process of photosynthesis in that the experiences of a particular individual in a particular place are consumed and transformed by the narrative imagination in order to use all available energy of those experiences: "The writer has attempted to write an absolutely true book to see whether the shape of a country and the pattern of a month's action can, if truly presented, compete with a work of the imagination" (*Green Hills*, foreword). The narrator moves from sickness to health as a result of his ability to perceive shape and pattern and to consume the meat of his experience.[6] What detractors of *Green Hills* fail to see is that the text is something other than an autobiographical account of Hemingway's African safari. *Green Hills* is a carefully imagined narrative about one individual's effort to discover "shape" and "pattern" in the relationship between his life and his physical environment.

As the story opens, an older, orthodox way of life is being rejected:

> We were sitting in the blind that Wanderobo hunters had built
> of twigs and branches at the edge of the salt-lick when we heard
> the truck coming. At first it was far away and no one could tell
> what the noise was. Then it moved slowly nearer, unmistakable
> now, louder and louder until, agonizing in a clank of loud irreg-
> ular explosions, it passed close behind us to go on up the road.
> The theatrical one of the two trackers stood up.
>   "It is finished," he said.
>   I put my hand to my mouth and motioned him down.
>   "It is finished," he said again and spread his arms wide.

In *The Nature of Narrative* Robert Scholes and Robert Kellogg observe
that for "western Narrative . . . the heterodox or personal symbol system has . . . tended to replace the orthodox." As Susan Lynn Drake
has demonstrated, *Green Hills of Africa* grapples with just such a re-
placement, documenting the death of the "orthodox" worldview and
heralding the coming of the "heterodox."[7]

Drake points out that "the larger background for this opening au-
gers a time of momentous change, for *Green Hills* is set in a continent
in motion. The narrative's African locale is caught up in a natural
turmoil, the imminent onslaught of the rainy season ('the rains were
moving north each day from Rhodesia')." This natural upheaval trig-
gers a social one—the migration of peoples along routes away from
the danger ("all along the road we passed groups of people making
their way to the westward"). Against this backdrop of change on con-
tinental, seasonal, and populational proportions, the narrative opens.

The narrator and hunting party have left their car to sit, waiting for
game, in a blind beside the road. As they wait another—failing—vehicle passes along the road. Its movement inspires one of the party to
get to his feet, arms outstretched and mouth open. In Drake's words,
"the elements of the vignette are few and stark, yet they resonate
through the narrative: the road, the blind, the two vehicles, the figure
that stands cruciate over the blind and the figure that curls within its
cavity." This crucial conjunction of forms enacts the moment of transition, when the narrator of *Green Hills*—the heterodox individual—and
a new world with him are born.

The opening presents the narrator in a fetal position: "The blind
had been built at close arrow-shot of the lick and sitting, leaning back,

knees high, heads low in a hollow half full of ashes and dust, watching through the dried leaves and thin branches I had seen a lesser kudu bull." The narrator's readiness for birth contrasts sharply with the poses of Garrick, the theatrical tracker, and the loud, irregular explosions of Kandisky's truck which brings an end to the day's hunt. "It is finished" are the first spoken words of the narrative and are general enough to permit reference to more than just the hunt or the engine of Kandisky's truck. Also finished is a way of life, one that is intellectual, European, and Christian.

The narrator's concern with what life does will contrast sharply with the older values embodied in the Christ-like words and pose of Garrick and in Kandisky's dislike of the modern world. Kandisky, for example, cannot use to extend his own skills the devices created by man's intellectual and imaginative powers; his is thus a way of life appropriately described as "finished": " 'Can we help?' I asked him. 'No,' he said. 'Unless you are a mechanic. It has taken a dislike to me. All engines dislike me. . . . Now I am afraid to make it go farther with that noise of death inside. It is trying to die because it dislikes me. Well, I dislike it too. But if I die it would not annoy it.' " Kandisky's lack of mechanical skill and corresponding willingness to see intention in the truck's difficulties reflect the attitude of an individual physically and imaginatively immobile. Not surprisingly, therefore, Kandisky sees himself as representing "European organization," the European characteristics reflected in his family of females, in his willingness to personify the truck, and in his sentiments about patriotism and society.[8] Because of his interest in poetry, Kandisky imagines that he and the individual he labels "Hemingway" (in the only place where the narrator is given this label) share an artistic temperament ("I see we have things in common"), but Kandisky sees art as only mental energy and makes careful distinctions between what he feels are the separate activities of an individual, aligning himself with the supposedly higher intellectual qualities rather than the grosser physical ones. Thus he shoots pictures rather than bullets (" 'I kill nothing, you understand' "), does not drink (" 'It's not good for the mind' "), and eagerly anticipates a safari " 'to study the natives.' " Above all, he values "the life of the mind": " 'I cannot buy new books now but we can always talk. Ideas and conversation are very interesting. We discuss all things. Everything. We have a very interesting mental life.' " But

Kandisky dissociates the mental life from the physical and sees the mental only in intellectual terms: " 'This is what I enjoy. This is the best part of life. The life of the mind. This is not killing kudu.' "

The interest of the protagonist/narrator also is the life of the mind, but he emphasizes life rather than mind and the activities and health of the mind rather than the stuffing of the mind with information. " 'These men . . . did not use the words that people always have used in speech, the words that survive in language. Nor would you gather that they had bodies. They had minds, yes. Nice, dry, clean minds.' " While Kandisky gathers information and support for his opinions, the narrator thinks not about the past but about his art. He values an art generated by an individual as alive to his physical skills as to his mental skills:

> "And what do you want?"
> "To write as well as I can and learn as I go along. . . ."
> "You really like to do this, what you do now, this silliness of kudu?"
> "Just as much as I like to be in the Prado."
> "One is not better than the other?"
> "One is as necessary as the other."

Kandisky fails to see the relationship between art and hunting. To Kandisky art is a creed, a goal for "Pursuit and Conversation." For the narrator, the value is not Art but a way of life; to hunt well or to write well is one and the same. To do anything well demands a total integration of skills. *Green Hills of Africa* is the expression of an individual's life of mind and of body, of a whole being seeking not to study life but to see what it can do and to be part of it. Kandisky categorizes life and lives in only one of its aspects. But the narrator seeks an art and a life expressive of each other. What is largely conversation in part 1 must be seen in relation to the completed text, a text which quite literally puts words into operation. The narrator, therefore, does what Nick Adams could not do and extends what Frederic Henry sought to do. Each of these narrators individually looks back in an effort to move forward.

Kandisky is not the only figure in the book contrasted with the narrator. Garrick, the tracker given to show rather than to talk, whose flamboyant gestures and assertive opinions mask his ignorance of both animals and hunting, and P.O.M., who embodies the characteristics of stability and comfort, are two such individuals. A third is Karl, the second hunter. Karl hunts, but he lacks the emotional and mental skills to hunt well. His kills are never clean; he overpowers an animal with four or five poorly placed shots. He comes back to camp with trophies, but his experience does not result in the satisfaction of having done something well. And in that discontent he isolates himself from everyone else. For him the camp provides only a place to eat and sleep between impassioned attacks upon the animals. For the narrator, whose wife accompanies him, the camp functions as a home, a place to restore powers that have dissipated during the activities of the day. He reads, enjoys a cool drink, talks over the hunt and art, and rests with his wife. While the coming rains impose an external limit on the time the narrator can hunt, Karl's limits are self-imposed, and he is thus always a little desperate: "I could believe it because of all people no one can be gentler, more understanding, more self-sacrificing, than Karl, but the kudu had become an obsession to him and he was not himself, nor anything like himself" (chap. 8). Significantly, Karl's activities do not contribute to health: "Karl was thin now, his skin sallow, his eyes very tired looking and he seemed a little desperate" (chap. 4).

Karl's complicated personal responses contrast sharply with the attitudes and activities of a group of characters who teach by example rather than precept. The book's last line—" 'I can remember him,' I said. 'I'll write you a piece some time and put him in' "—suggests that the germ of the narrative grows, as biologically it should, out of Pop, a father figure who combines experience with authority and teaching. Pop stimulates, but the narrator carries that stimulation within himself and therefore usually hunts without Pop. The narrator returns to Pop to talk over a hunt or an idea, but he hunts with others, individuals like Kamau, Droopy, M'Cola, and the Masai tribesmen, who embody the clean skills that get so completely lost in Karl's complicated attitude. "Kamau was very modest, quiet, and an excellent driver and now, as we came out of the bush country, and into an open, scrubby, desert-looking stretch, I looked at him, whose elegance, achieved with an old coat and a safety pin, whose modesty, pleasantness and skill I admired so much" (chap. 10). Garrick's gestures and Kandisky's sentiments look and sound good, but *Green Hills of Africa* values the ability to function, a quality that has no need to call attention to itself:

"M'Cola was not jealous of Droopy. He simply knew that Droop was a better man than he was. More of a hunter, a faster and a cleaner tracker, and a great stylist in everything he did" (chap. 3).

The narrator's organization of material in *Green Hills* indicates that, whatever the original experience, he has come to see the characters of his story in terms of shape and pattern; he can imagine and verbalize their individual actions within an overall narrative structure. *Green Hills*, therefore, is not an intellectual exercise in learning to hunt or an account of the physical experience of getting a kudu or a discussion of aesthetics. Rather, it integrates all these activities in one healthy individual who has learned to see shape and pattern and has developed the ability to function—to write, live, and hunt—cleanly. The image in which these values center is that of the Gulf Stream:

> That stream will flow, as it has flowed . . . after the Americans and after all the Cubans and all the systems of governments, the richness, the poverty, the martyrdom, the sacrifice and the venality and the cruelty are all gone as the high-piled scow of garbage, bright-colored, white-flecked, ill-smelling, now tilted on its side, spills off its load into the blue water, turning it a pale green to a depth of four or five fathoms as the load spreads across the surface . . . the stream, with no visible flow, takes five loads of this a day when things are going well in La Habana and in ten miles along the coast it is as clear and blue and unimpressed as it was ever before the tug hauled out the scow; and the palm fronds of our victories, the worn light bulbs of our discoveries and the empty condoms of our great loves float with no significance against one single, lasting thing—the stream. (chap. 8)

The qualities of the stream are "permanent and of value" because it is a moving force capable of continual self-purification. Similarly, an individual's imaginative activities—if he is not Kandisky or Karl—purge old ideas, stultifying sentiments, and complicated patterns of life, making possible renewal and growth.

Like the Gulf Stream, the narrative effort in *Green Hills* is to purify and initiate movement: "I had been quite ill and had that pleasant feeling of getting stronger each day." The physical cleansing is not in itself sufficient; the emotions must be purged of competitive jealousies and personal self-centeredness. Thus part 2, "Pursuit Remembered," introduces Karl and centers on the competition between the two American hunters. The narrator knows that he himself is the better shot, but trophy dominates skill in his mind until he can put Karl and all that Karl stimulates away from him. Part 2 ends with Karl's leaving camp for sable country while the narrator continues his hunt for kudu; the physical separation of the two men is only one indication, however, that the complicating emotions associated with Karl have been cleansed. In his narration of the second part, it is clear that the narrator has developed the ability to see himself and Karl through eyes unclouded by frustration or anger:

> Karl and I out on the plain in the too much sun and dust had gone through one of those rows that starts like this, "What was the matter?"
> "They were too far."
> "Not at the start."
> "They were too far, I tell you."
> "They get hard if you don't take them."
> "You shoot them."
> "I've got enough. . . . You go ahead."
> Then some one, angry, shooting too fast to show he was being asked to shoot too fast, getting up from behind the ant hill and turning away in disgust, walking toward his partner, who says, smugly, "What's the matter with them?"
> "They're too damned far, I tell you," desperately.
> The smug one, complacently, "Look at them."

That the dialogue in this passage is hypothetical and that the narrator can see his own smugness attest to the objectivity achieved in contrast to the passion that overwhelms vision and judgment. He sees Karl's weaknesses, but, more importantly, he sees his own and the resulting complicated atmosphere that prevents good hunting. He sees this with a control as necessary to hunting as to writing: "I was watching, freezing myself deliberately inside, stopping the excitement as you close a valve, going into that impersonal state you shoot from."

The narrator's improving health becomes evident also in his increasing interest in books. He has as yet no compulsion to read or write, but he directs much of his attention in the second section to books, in particular to those of Tolstoi. The narrator responds to two qualities in Tolstoi's *Sevastopol*: the fighting and the ability to perceive a physical world. For a writer like Tolstoi the "great advantage [of] an experience of war" is that it teaches economy. War shatters ideals and theories because it subjects them to the test of painful experience in which the only emerging value is life. A writer can then work with the one subject genuinely concrete and can do so with the necessary economy that strips away rhetorical flourishes. In contrast to the "old timer" with "eyes used to vast distances," the narrative eye able to see cleanly works alone and with objectivity, focusing on the natural world, and, therefore, objects rather than abstractions or symbols fascinate. In Tolstoi's "The Cossacks," for example, "were the summer heat, the mosquitoes, the feel of the forest in the different seasons, and that river that the Tartars crossed."

Earlier, when his physical health was the most immediate concern, the narrator "read with no obligation and no compulsion to write." Physically stronger, he now rediscovers his interest in writing: "To work was the only thing, it was the one thing that always made you feel good." Living well physically is not enough; the intellectual and imaginative faculties must develop as well. The drive to function as a fully integrated being—to *work* in the scientific sense of the word—centers in the hunt for the kudu, whose importance as the object of the hunt is imaged in its heart-shaped track. The heart as the center of life—not, as in the nineteenth-century view, the center of feeling—is the direction in which the narrator has been moving from the beginning. He drives not to grasp or to destroy that life but to participate in it. Kandisky seeks to study life, Karl, to take it home as a trophy, but the narrator, in the final chapter, wants to function as an alive being in a living world: "I did not mind killing anything, any animal, if I killed it cleanly, they all had to die and my interference with the nightly and seasonal killing that went on all the time was very minute and I had no guilty feeling at all. We ate the meat and kept the hides and horns." His killing is part of an ongoing process, for a living organism must kill in order to live. An artist's consuming living material and transforming it into his own life manifest that same process, a process at work as well in the green of Africa's hills and in the narrator's killing of kudu. A herbivore, the kudu consumes green vegetation. As carnivore, the hunter kills the herbivore and eats its purifying organs. Not an intruder, he participates in the chain of life initiated by the energy of the sun. The killing of the kudu, however, does not end the process;

eating the kudu signals health and the possibility of growth, the stimulation of the imaginative powers, and the concern, expressed in the
book's last sentence, for creating *Green Hills of Africa*. That creative act
also involves consumption, of the experiences and lives of those beings who participated in the two-month safari in Africa. In a very real
sense, therefore, the book is not *about* life but is the *product* of a living
act.

One other characteristic of the kudu, according to Pop, is that it is
hunted alone, and the narrator has indicated that good writing demands working alone. Part 3 ends when the report of a virgin country
makes possible on this safari one last chance to get a kudu. Leaving
P.O.M. (wife) and Pop (father), the narrator strikes out for new country. "I looked back as we went down the hill and saw the two figures,
the tall thick one and the small neat one, each wearing big Stetson
hats, silhouetted on the road as they walked back toward camp, then I
looked ahead at the dried-up, scrubby plain."

The new country and the people who live there initially present to
the narrator a living creature not to be killed but to be touched: "They
caught the rabbit and the tallest runner came up with him to the car
and handed him to me. I held him and could feel the thumping of his
heart through the soft, warm, furry body." After meeting the magnificent Masai tribesmen, the narrator encounters natives he had never
seen before, dressed in what look like Roman togas: "Their faces were
a gray brown, the oldest looked to be about fifty, had thin lips, an
almost Grecian nose, rather high cheekbones, and large, intelligent
eyes." The natives will serve as guides for the kudu kill, the final act of
purification, and their ancient characteristics (Greek nose and Roman
toga) suggest their part in the long purification process. Like part 2,
a narrative trip back in order to make possible the narrative movement
forward, the presence of these natives suggests that the sources have
been reached and that the complicating patterns of behavior and
emotional turmoils have ended. Appropriately, therefore, when they
leave camp the final time before shooting kudu, they leave Garrick
and his theatrics behind.

The narrator kills two kudu cleanly, shooting just twice. "He was
lying on the side where the bullet had gone in and there was not a
mark on him and he smelled sweet and lovely like the breath of cattle
and the odor of thyme after rain." Much of the description early in the

book was given to the dust and heat and famine of the country and to the stench of the animals, in particular the baboons and the hyenas who fed on death. With the kudu it is different, as though the narrator has truly moved as far as he can into the clean new world, where the Romans and Masai now accept him as an equal. Before the kill he tried to use a dictionary to communicate; now there is no need for common verbal language: "We were all hunters except, possibly, Garrick, and the whole thing could be worked out, understood, and agreed to without using anything but a forefinger to signal and a hand to caution."

A romantic and quite untrue story might end with the kudu kill, but *Green Hills* stresses process rather than goal. The first twelve chapters narrate the story of the narrator's drive to achieve a unification of his powers, a drive that carries him into new country and into relationships based upon skill rather than need. The final chapter is, quite literally, the trip back, back to Pop and P.O.M. and Karl, but with new perceptions and as a whole being. He will now be able to work well—to write, for example, *Green Hills*—in a world of dust and heat and mosquitoes.

As part of this trip back, the sable hunt is crucial, for during this hunt the narrator becomes aware of his weaknesses and accepts the responsibility for them as well as for his strengths. Garrick once again hunts with them, making the narrator nervous, but he ultimately takes responsibility for the gut-shot animal: "If I'd gone to bed last night I would not have done that. Or if I'd wiped out the bore to get the oil out she would not have thrown high the first time. Then I would not have pulled down and shot under her the second shot. Every damned thing is your own fault if you're any good." This is not only an acceptance of his fault but also a statement of the fact that he is good. During the book he has become good, a healthy individual, and that demands awareness of his responsibility for what fails as well as for what succeeds. When he returns to Pop and P.O.M. to discover that once again Karl has beaten him—using four or five shots to do it—the complicating emotions reappear only to be accepted and put aside:

> But I was bitter and I was bitter all night long. In the morning, though, it was gone. It was all gone and I have never had it again. . . .

"I'm really glad he has him," I said truly. "Mine'll hold me."

"We have very primitive emotions," [Pop] said. "It's impossible not to be competitive. Spoils everything, though."

"I'm all through with that," I said. "I'm all right again. I had quite a trip, you know."

It has been quite a trip, a trip to end narrative and personal division and to become, in the fullest sense of the word, "articulate," verbally and physically mobile. The narrator cuts loose from enclosures that separate an individual from his environment and seeks to grow with those patterns inherent in the natural world. The extraordinary integration within the text of imagery, character, dialogue, pattern of action, and setting is a remarkable achievement. In its effort to initiate individual growth by interrelating patterns of a personal life and its particular physical environment, *Green Hills of Africa* is a most western of narratives.

5

The Big Sky:
Searching for a New Story

When A. B. Guthrie, Jr., wrote an introduction for Lewis Garrard's *Wah-to-yah and the Taos Trail*, he noted Garrard's enjoyment of western life. Garrard, says Guthrie, "not only liked the rude and unfettered life of the frontier; he liked his companions, the traders, the mountain men, the bucks and squaws and papooses." That same liking for the land and its people finds expression in Guthrie's own work. A comparison of Jack Schaeffer's *Shane* to Guthrie's screenplay of the same novel, for example, dramatically calls attention to the difference between the easterner Schaeffer's commitment to talk and character development and the westerner Guthrie's focus on the land. Guthrie, born in 1901, was raised in Choteau, Montana, the area of the "big sky" given prominence in all his work. Schaeffer's is not a visual narrative; the physical world is relatively unimportant. In contrast, *The Big Sky* (1947), Guthrie's best-known novel, demonstrates liking for the land complicated by an overwhelming concern for the future. In the hands of a weaker writer, that combination could lead to nostalgia and lament; Guthrie's art, however, produces a work impressive in its depiction of the forces that can close down an individual's effort to break free of enclosures.

Both *Shane* and *The Big Sky* are stories of generational and cultural transfer. *Shane*'s eastern orientation—Jack Schaeffer had never been west of Ohio when he wrote the book—is evident in the fact that it encloses the image of the heroic Shane within a child's voice, that of the narrator, Bobby Starrett. The beauty of "Shane" is quite literally, then, a child's dream. Schaeffer reinforces the cultural shift from Shane's gunfighting world to Joe Starrett's farming world by giving the narrative point of view to the young boy. What that boy narrates is the idea he has always carried within him, the idea he calls "Shane." He concludes: "But when they talked like that, I simply smiled because I knew [Shane] could have been none of these. He was the man who rode into our little valley out of the heart of the great glowing West and when his work was done rode back whence he had come and he was Shane."

The Big Sky also focuses on change, represented both by the closing world of the mountain men and by the youthful Boone Caudill replacing Dick Summers and Uncle Zeb. The narrator, like Bob Starrett, does look back to a lost beauty, but his vision is situational rather than nostalgic. The narrator is concerned with a moment in history when power was transferred, a moment that forces us to look toward and to question the emergence of a new story. *Shane* is interested not in the story of Bob Starrett but only in his remembrance of Shane. Cultures change in *Shane*, but the focus of subsequent generations continues to be the glories of the old. In contrast, *The Big Sky* concentrates on Boone Caudill's inability to form his own story, on his inability to give himself direction and motion: "For a while Summers could see Boone, weaving big and dark into the darkness, and then he couldn't see him any more, and he turned and went back into the cabin." The last of the mountain men, Dick Summers retreats here in the novel's final words to an enclosure, while Boone, the new generation, disappears into darkness. The book seeks to understand this transfer of power. But it is a book whose ending is troubled.

Like Nathaniel Hawthorne's *The Scarlet Letter* or Henry James's *The Portrait of a Lady*, *The Big Sky* opens with the confrontation between a world of enclosure and the violation of that world. In canonical writings such violation frequently leads to new enclosures—James, for example, develops defined characters who can function within the social structure. In the popular westerns of Louis L'Amour or Ernest Haycox or Max Brand, this confrontation usually involves exaggeratedly virile men who impose themselves on the land. That none of these possibilities occurs in *The Big Sky* frequently generates irritation that Boone does not grow or the sense that the story does not lead anywhere. But Guthrie's is a book not of individuals but of forces, forces that are both initiated by Boone and that put Boone into motion. The causes and direction of that motion become the subjects of the book. Neither the individual nor the land is central—in fact the land is strikingly indifferent to events; it provides a stability within which the forces operate. The book does not "arrive" anywhere because, as Dick Summers says, you can live on the land but learning to work it, to wrestle it into the shape you want, reduces a man to exhaustion. Not a book, therefore, with a message for future settlement, *The Big Sky* presents a vision of man as a transient rather than a transforming presence. Not a book that illustrates an idea or that arrives at a conclusion, it instead looks at a particular moment with an eye to the forces working within the moment.[1] Boone's story has the ingredients for discovery, but his final destructive act—killing his friend and companion, Jim Deakins—does not free him to new possibility; instead, the killing dooms him to wandering in darkness.

In contrast to *Wah-to-yah and the Taos Trail* or *The Land of Little Rain*, which break away from the enclosing form of the East, *The Big Sky* has a highly controlled structure. The story is presented in five parts— "1830," "1830," "1837," "1843–1843," "1843"—and its structure calls attention, first, to a fascination with time and, second, to a concern with balance. Parts 1 and 2 balance 4 and 5, each focusing on a particular year. Part 3 works as a pivot, forming either of two units depending on whether it completes parts 1 and 2 or it initiates parts 4 and 5. In other words, part 3 integrates both the story of Boone's explosion out of confinement into union with the Indian Teal Eye and the story of an Edenic impulse that becomes self-destructive at the end of part 4.

The book's structure, therefore, works to interlock the five sections of the narrative, producing an atmosphere of inevitability that lends itself well to the tragic (in its classical sense) proportions of the story. The use of a date for the title of each section reinforces this overarching sense of fatality. Boone Caudill, embodying the traditional American story of the young man who breaks free from authority to discover possibility in the West, is thus never his own agent. Dominating his actions are not eastern establishment and western violence but land and time, a domination reflected in the interlocking sections of the narrative. Boone is not free to leave behind part 1 as he moves to part 2, in spite of the fact that parts 1 and 2 are distinct entities. It is certainly inviting to see part 1 as closing with Boone's frustration with confinement and part 2 as opening with opportunities in new physical territory. But Boone cannot leave the first and enter the second because the two are united by the title "1830," because they are both stories of threat that thrust Boone into new experience, and because together with part 3 they form a unit that culminates Boone's drive to unite with Teal Eye. The separation of the sections implies the possibility of a break with previous events, but the controlling interlock denies that possibility. The tension between these forces provides the dynamics of the narrative.

The richness of *The Big Sky* results from multiple interactions of contradictory themes, which push the book forward toward the possibility of a new story but which simultaneously destroy that possibility. Part 1 ("1830") establishes the world to be rejected and the forces to be carried forward, whereas part 5 brings us back to the rejected world, implying that few if any alternatives actually exist. The overpowering characteristic of the world established in part 1 is enclosure. Like the opening of *Huck Finn*, Guthrie's first section presents a young man confined by buildings, family, society, and systems. The story opens inside the Caudill house as the father, John Caudill, enters yelling, "Where's Boone?" Boone is outside and not anxious to enter because he knows that Pap represents threat. Throughout the narrative, Boone will be outside, trying to avoid the threat of enclosure and authority. Pap beats Boone, and Boone lashes out; the law, in a later chapter of this first part, also beats Boone, and again he lashes out.

In part 1 confinement extends beyond father and legal system; Boone's entire world, social and physical, seeks to impose its terms. His chance encounter with Jonathan Bedwell, a stranger with whom Boone shares his food, leads first to the theft of his prize gun and later to imprisonment. An entire town chases him; even "words came at Boone again, like rocks being pitched" by a court system characterized by its cruelty and comedy, both of which undercut its authority. When Boone is on the road, the "trees hunched close around him," and mist cuts off his vision. Buildings—tollhouses—exact fees for traveling through the land and must be avoided. Even the many pages given to depicting Boone's trial act as a weight that verbally denies any possibility to realizing his longing for the world outside. Toward the end of the section, his prosecutor comments that he is "probably a bound boy" and ought to be held for investigation, a statement that nicely describes all the bonds engulfing Boone.

Part 1, however, does more than set up a contrast between the urges of the young person and the constricting adult world. Though that contrast is the focus of the section, established as well is the part that Boone plays within this world. The opening scene has the father call out for Boone, yell at him because a warrant has been issued for his arrest, and then attempt to beat him because he had been fighting with Mose Napier. Boone rebels, but we must remember he is fighting his own father; this is family, and family (genetics) will haunt Boone. He returns in part 5 in response to a letter from his mother, but that return is actually in response to more than the letter. Together with Teal Eye, Boone has produced a son who has red hair and is blind. In part 4 the discovery of these two traits, particularly the red hair, convinces Boone that the father is really his friend, Jim Deakins. But in part 5 Boone finds that these traits also run in his family, a discovery that underscores the blindness he figuratively shares with his son. Quite literally, then, it is less the external physical threats from which he seeks to remove himself than the seeds within Boone himself that destroy him. When part 1 ends, the implication is that the numerous threats of the opening—familial, legal, social—end also; a new beginning starts with part 2. But Boone carries the seeds of part 1 inside him. Given that presentation, Boone's return in part 5 becomes a necessity.

An important scene in part 1 embodying both the impulse toward new life and the forces of inevitable destruction occurs on the road just after Boone has run away: " 'Goin' to Louisville myself,' the driver said. 'Wisht I could make her afore night, but it ain't no use. Time don't mean nothin' to a dead man, no more'n to a hog, but seems like it means a heap to his kin.' He jerked his thumb toward the back of the wagon, and Boone, looking over his shoulder, saw a plank box there." Jim Deakins, the driver, will be a major figure in the narrative not simply because he remains Boone's companion until Boone kills him in part 4 but also because Jim's reappearances always occasion a corpse. In part 1 it is the body of the elderly gentleman; in part 4 he bears news of coming settlement and, at the end of the section, a letter for Boone from his mother. As a white, easterner, talker, and man of ideas, Jim has the potential to destroy. He needs the spontaneity of Boone, and Boone needs the intellect of Jim. They work well *together*. When they initially meet here in part 1, Boone has just beaten his father and is trying to get away from the confinement his father's world embodies; Jim carries the corpse of an elderly father who has had a farm, five wives, and innumerable children—strong ties to settlement. In one sense that father figure is being buried as Boone strikes out for new opportunities; in another, of course, it trails along behind.

Chronologically, part 2 immediately follows the close of part 1. Boone has just gotten his revenge on Sheriff York and put his father, family, and the East behind. Part 2 is the new beginning, a movement into a land as lovely as a "virgin woman" and a clean break from the confinement of part 1. This section introduces the big sky, a world in which one could see forever. "It made a man little and still big, like a king looking out. It occurred to Boone that this was the way a bird must feel, free and loose, with the world to choose from." It is also buffalo country and presents as well a long list of such new foods as dog, beaver, "painter," snake, and even man. The crew of the *Mandan* initiates Boone and Jim as they cross the Platte for the first time, and Dick Summers appears as Boone's guide. We have, in other words, all the ingredients for breaking loose and the possibility of discovery. Even a lovely young Indian girl accompanies the crew as it struggles west into the virgin land.[2]

Teal Eye, the young girl, is named for the beauty of her eyes. In a country that invites one to "see forever" and a story in which Boone's son will be born blind, Teal Eye—Indian, virginal, and visually alert—has special qualities. The whites are bringing her back to her father, in a seeming inversion of the Pocahontas story, but their intentions are not those of caring or concern. The whites, distinctively European descendants in language and song, have a plan that reminds us that the move west does not always break new ground but rather extends the eastern impulse for profit: Teal Eye will be used to open markets with the Blackfeet Indians. The young girl's eyes stimulate interest, but none of the males sees her as anything other than a sexual object or monetary investment.

The virgin land welcomes the male thrust; groans of sexual pleasure become the dominant early sounds of part 2, causing one Indian chief to ask if no women exist where the whites come from. The West is fertile and receptive, open to penetration. New foods, new sights, new demands lead to Boone's sense of feeling "the way a bird must feel." "The heart big and urgent in the throat" expresses equally the desire for women and the lushness of the land. But the crew had simi-

lar yearnings in St. Louis for whores, and consequently Boone has
syphilis. Dick Summers tells Boone not to worry because they have all
had it; it goes away. Perhaps the symptoms disappear, but the disease
does not; as these males thrust themselves into lush, willing Indian
women, they leave behind the disease. At the end of the book, Dick
tells Boone that "everything we done it looks like we done against
ourselves."

In part 1 Jim Deakins carried one corpse with him; when the *Mandan* struggles west, it carries two out of St. Louis. Though the bodies
are buried and the boat pushes on against the violent current and tor-
rential rains, these bodies and Boone's syphilis undercut the possibility of the break offered between parts 1 and 2. Part 2 does develop
the potential inherent in rejecting confinement, but it also carries forward the implications of seeds, particularly sperm, being planted.
As it must, because of the nature of planted seeds, part 2 concludes
with violence rising out of the wilderness to attack, to obliterate the
intended plans of the East.

Dick and Jim save Boone from the slaughter, and together the three
continue west. Part 3 ends with the union of Boone and Teal Eye. The
text jumps in part 3 seven years to 1837, with that section opening as a
peaceful contrast to the violence that closed part 2: "The wind was
warm, coming over the mountains, and notionable. Sometimes it cried
shrill and wintry in the branches of the trees and then it would ease up
and be no more than a whisper that the ear wouldn't catch unless it
listened. . . . By and by sleep would come on him again, and the wind
would be like a river flowing, running along with his dreams." Both
time and mood indicate a sharp break with the unit that integrated
parts 1 and 2. In each of those, Boone exploded out of confining systems into a potentially new world. With part 3 the potential for growth
seems to have become a reality as Boone, under the example of Dick
Summers, has learned to be a trapper and hunter. Dick's influence
diminishes until midway through part 3, when he retires from the
West, and Boone's independence correspondingly increases. Once
again, therefore, a pattern is established that suggests possibility. And
as before, the pattern is undercut in subsequent action.

Occurring at the center both of part 3 and of the book itself is the
episode of the trappers' rendezvous, the annual gathering of mountain men who sell their furs, buy supplies for the coming year, and

generally work off pent-up energies. In a narrative that has been moving away from the confinement, comedy, and cruelty of the eastern
legal system, this gathering of mountain men at the very center of
the text provides an opportunity to depict a contrasting system of values. But the rendezvous turns into a drunken orgy with its own cruelty. Boone kills Streak, another mountain man, in an argument over
the Indian Poordevil, an act that his companions see as proving his
manhood but that otherwise has no meaning to them. Poordevil lifts
Streak's scalp, and the incident is forgotten. We thus are provided two
alternative gatherings of men in *The Big Sky*: the law in Louisville or
the rendezvous out west. Whether we reject the first for the second or
look to the first to stabilize the world of the second, we are trapped;
both see white men as collectively destructive.

The alternative to either unattractive gathering is the land and the
individual freed from confinement, discovering his own potential.
Boone, however, is troubling in this role both because of the syphilis within and his own vicious impulses in killing Streak and, importantly, because Boone lacks the vision of Dick or the speculative incli-
nations of Jim. Dick Summers recognizes that Boone doesn't "know
how to get around a thing," but worse is Boone's inability to read the
signs of his own environment.[3] The incidents of part 3 occur in 1837,
at the time when the life of the mountain man was closing. Beaver
was disappearing, and the East would soon be more fascinated with
silk hats than with beaver. Dick and Boone's Uncle Zeb recognize the
situation, but Boone cannot:

> A body got so's he felt everything was kin to him, the earth and
> sky and buffalo and beaver and the yellow moon at night. It was
> better than being walled in by a house. . . . Here a man lived
> natural. Some day, maybe, it would all end, as Summers said it
> would, but not any ways soon—not so soon a body had to look
> ahead. . . . The country was too wild and cold for settlers.
> Things went up and down and up again. Everything did. Beaver
> would come back, and fat prices, and the good times that old
> men said were going forever.

So Boone himself, the only alternative to the systems provided by the
book, establishes potential problems. Perhaps that explains, in part,
Boone's drive toward Teal Eye, the desire to unite his self-sufficiency
with her eyes, her ability to see.

Boone's desire for Teal Eye becomes the focus of the novel's second half. The rendezvous culminates the drive toward "freedom" in a new world, and Dick Summers leaves. With that as the story of the first half, the second focuses on Boone and Teal Eye, but their union does not fulfill the promise of a new story. An apparent alternative to the implications of the book's first half, the second only returns us, in part 5, to the opening. Given the contradictions Boone carries within, there is really no alternative.

Part 3 closes with Boone's rediscovery of Teal Eye, but between the rendezvous and the rediscovery appear troubling events, the most obvious of which are the killing of the Crow Indian as Boone seeks a prize horse to present as payment for Teal Eye and the encountering of the Indian village decimated by white man's smallpox: " 'White man bring whisky,' Poordevil translated. 'Make Injun crazy. White man sleep with squaw. Make sick here.' His hand went to his crotch. 'White man heart bad. . . . Keep white man away. White man bring big medicine, big sickness.' "

Less obvious than these warning signs but perhaps more important is the fact that Boone seems to live in a dream world, embodied in Teal Eye, and fails to see the killing and disease he brings with him. Responding to Poordevil's report of Indian woes, Boone says, " 'Tell him it's the French and not the Long Knives.' "

Boone finds his Eden during the five years that separate parts 3 and 4, five years of living with Teal Eye as an Indian: "One day and another it was pretty much the same, and it was all good. . . . Life went along one day after another as it had for five seasons now, and the days went together and lost themselves in one another. . . . It was all he could ask, just to be living like this, with his belly satisfied and himself free and his mind peaceful and in his lodge a woman to suit him." Boone has found his answer to the confinement of part 1, but confinement also becomes his answer, for it is decidedly Edenic, suggesting that perhaps the drives that have impelled Boone from the beginning are drives not toward freedom and possibility but from a world in which he is not comfortable.

Jim Deakins soon reappears bearing corpses—news of settlement (and, therefore, dying worlds) and, later, news that Boone's father has died. That part 4 integrates the Edenic opening, the killing of Jim Deakins, and the rejection of Teal Eye suggests once again that all the drives in the novel are integrated. The major incidents of part 4 describe Boone serving as guide to an entrepreneur, Elisha Peabody, but not as a Dick Summers revealing knowledge in a virgin wilderness. Peabody appreciates western beauty but even more the possibility of erecting a tollhouse in the pass through which new settlers will have to travel. Not surprisingly, when Boone shoots Jim, we are told that "closed in by walls, the pistol sounded big." Boone's flight from walls comes to an end with he himself reasserting them.

Part 5 begins where it must, with Boone returning home. Once again confinement asserts itself in the flow of words, conflicts, and games people play with one another, together smothering house and family, even the natural terrain: "But now he felt different, cramped by the forest that rose thick as grass over him, shutting out the sun and letting him see only a piece of sky now and then, and it faded and closed down like a roof. The wind was dead here; not even the leaves of the great poplars, rising high over all the rest, so much as trembled. It was a still, closed-in, broody world, and a man in it went empty and lost inside . . . And all living smothered by walls and roofs, breathing air that the good was gone from, breathing each other's stinks." This world is moving west—the caravans of men tied like mules to their families, the minister who feels that the Indians need the white man's God, perhaps even the homesteader who beats his dog to make him conform.

Of course, Boone doesn't fit in this environment, even though his genes place him here. And he doesn't fit out west, where his genes bring blindness and destruction. The last action in the book is exerted by Dick Summers, whom Boone briefly visits before again turning westward. "For a while Summers could see Boone, weaving big and dark into the darkness, and then he couldn't see him any more, and he turned and went back into the cabin. There was cold corn pone on the table, and cold poke greens and a ham butt and a pitcher of buttermilk. His woman had gone to bed, she tired so easy these days." Whatever the West offered, this aging mountain man finds solace in enclosure.

The Big Sky does not celebrate the West or the virgin land or the passing of the mountain man. Always, the West is less the object of attention than the field on which the narrative works out the forces initiated in the opening. The field is attractive in itself, but it is more omnipresent than present, as though it has existed for millions of years and will endure for millions more. The book focuses on this surface where men of potential breed their own destruction.

An easterner might tell a similar story, but his would be one of conflicting ideas. "The Bear" sequence of William Faulkner's *Go Down, Moses,* for example, focuses on the land but largely as subject for the intellectual positions of Ike McCaslin and Roth Edmonds. More like Caddy Compson (who flees Faulkner's world) in *The Sound and the Fury* than Ike McCaslin, Boone Caudill is attracted to new land, where he struggles to find his own place and story. He is unsuccessful; but even as part 4 of *The Big Sky* turns back to part 5, as Boone wanders off into the dark and as Dick settles for enclosure, the narrative works forward. We do not end the book with a lament for Boone—he is not that likable—or for the land—we have not seen that much of it. We end rather with a sense of a story that has struggled against and within the constrictions of its own form.

The Big Sky narrates the effort of this impulse to break free from enclosures into a land open to opportunity, but that effort works within a textual structure that continually checks the impulse. In this, *The Big Sky* reverses Charles Brockden Brown's *Wieland,* where the narrative impulse struggles to close a structure that keeps trying to open. The impulse in Guthrie's novel is crucial to defining its place in American writing, for the forces holding back that impulse are part of Boone Caudill's past and the enclosures of tradition. Boone's world closes down on him, but his effort toward new life in a new land remains very much alive within the experience of the novel.

6

High Country in *The Ox-Bow Incident*

Perhaps the most common story in western writing is the border story. Spatially, border stories happen at places like the Texas-Mexico border; temporally, borders are set at critical turning points such as the 1840s in *The Big Sky* or the 1880s in *The Ox-Bow Incident*. The border story is certainly not the special province of the West—*Wieland, The Scarlet Letter*, and "The Open Boat" are eastern border stories—but when an easterner uses the border form, he perceives the border as a frontier dividing warring states or environments. In William Byrd's *History of the Dividing Line* or William Dean Howells's *Hazard of New Fortunes* (in the figure of Jacob Dryfoos), for example, the wilderness world is a fixed quantity to be walled out or ended. So also in the popular western, itself the product of an eastern imagination, though in these stories of the frontier, the savage world across the border or outside the walls of the fort can never be completely walled out but remains a constant threat to civilization. Not surprisingly, the border in the popular western writing of Zane Grey or Louis L'Amour is usually spatial, for internal change is not an issue; values have already been culturally delineated. It is appropriate that in its heyday the popular western movie was filmed in black and white, a contrast that mirrored the clean borders of the story.

Clear distinctions in popular western border novels, however, become significantly blurred in the hands of such writers as A. B. Guthrie, Jr., Walter Van Tilburg Clark, and Harvey Fergusson. No longer is it a case of the good guys in the fort versus the savages outside screaming for blood. The border in these stories becomes a "frontier" in the sense of a place of transition rather than demarcation. This new frontier describes, therefore, an area of continual opening.

Because the western writer does not see the individual as an ego distinct from his environment, he perceives little reward in looking inward in order to understand the self and instead places the self in relation to an external world possessing its own order and savagery. In effect, the western writer says that "nature is, after all, a part of what we are. There is little to be gained living separately." One novel that uses the images of borders in particularly effective ways is Walter Van Tilburg Clark's *The Ox-Bow Incident* (1940).[1]

James Fenimore Cooper set *The Last of the Mohicans* in 1757, the time of the French and Indian Wars; like Cooper, Guthrie and Vardis Fisher in their novels of the mountain men focus on the end of an era and the beginnings of western settlement. Walter Clark is equally careful with the temporal and spatial borders in *Ox-Bow*. The year is the spring of 1885; the town is Bridger's Wells. In general terms, 1885 can serve as a cutoff date for the West of cowboys, Indians, cattle drives, and outlaws. The disastrous winter of 1885–86 destroyed herds and marked, notes Henry Nash Smith, "the real end of the frontier period."[2] Jim Bridger was by many accounts the greatest of the mountain men and later became a trader and guide for settlement wagon trains. Consequently, 1885 in Bridger's Wells sets *Ox-Bow* at a major point of transition between the reality of the Old West and the myth that was to begin with the story of Buck Taylor in 1887. When Art Croft and Gil Carter arrive in Bridger's Wells, their first visit is to the saloon, where behind the bar is prominently displayed a painting of a seminude "woman who was no girl any longer." In Clark's novel, the West has outgrown its youth, and problems of maturation become the subject.

The temporal border, then, is the year 1885; the spatial border lies between Bridger's Wells and the mountains out of which ride the narrator, Art Croft, and his winter sidekick. When the town's posse forms to hunt rustlers, it rides into the mountains, the high country, where three lynchings take place. The novel concerns itself with the impulses that govern civilized/natural man; the story becomes the effort of Art Croft to read, organize, and unify this border world. But Art is a reluctant narrator, both of his own story and of the stories of others—he says in the concluding scene, "Why in hell, I wondered, did everybody have to take me for his father confessor?"

Critics' discussions of "meaning" in *The Ox-Bow Incident* have frequently centered on such matters as demagoguery and mob psychology. Clark himself added to this way of dealing with the novel when he spoke topically of the 1940 story in the context of Nazism. Much of the novel is certainly given to "meaning," but to see the book as a study of ideas focuses attention on qualities external to the narrative and ultimately presents a rather flat idea book.[3] What readers of *Ox-Bow* do in concentrating on meaning is similar to what the characters within the novel do: everyone spends a great deal of time analyzing the situation, and consequently they lose sight of the forces that drive the text. Meaning, while an aspect of the book, is less important as a message one takes from the novel than as playing a destructive role within the novel.

To understand both the effort of the narrative and its outcome, we need to concern ourselves with the narrator, Art Croft. Although no commentator, to my knowledge, has called attention to Art's name, the relationship between "Art Croft" and "Art Craft" or "the Craft of Art" seems clear. The relationship should not be slighted. The western imagination works within an environment from which the enclosures of the East have been removed. That effort sets up exciting imaginative possibilities. Almost as interesting as the possibilities are the failures, for they point the way of the struggle. In these terms, Art Croft's reluctance to integrate his Art is central to defining what the western imagination seeks to do.[4]

Art Croft's story of a group of distinct individuals who try to unite to end a threat to their jobs and lives is one that implicitly values union and function. Left to themselves, the men would begin fighting or would drift off in separate directions. They come together, however, to effect change within a very particular social and natural environment. As character, Art Croft participates in this collective effort; as narrator, he seeks to integrate disparate emotions, ideas, and motivations into a working narrative. But both efforts break down. The posse becomes a lynch mob, and the narrative disintegrates in the final scene into a jumble of voices. Whatever his impulses, Art finally settles for being an observer, an individual who trusts language to convey a message, rather than being an explorer of narrative and relationship.[5]

In 1885 Bridger's Wells sits in the past, a town "beginning to settle into a half-empty village" of boarded-up buildings with cracked paint and a scattering of dying poplars. The story, however, opens in the spring: "It was good to be on the loose on that kind of a day, but winter range stores up a lot of things in a man, and spring roundup hadn't worked them all out." The image of two young men riding out of winter hibernation unites natural and human physical energies. So *Ox-Bow* is put into motion by energy anxious to become active in a world whose past reason for existence is rapidly decaying. Though *Ox-Bow* begins with spring, initiating the effort of Art/"Art" to integrate potentially discordant impulses into the thrust of new life, the book finally tells a story of death. And we are left with a concern for what goes wrong, why the thwarted impulse.

Art and Gil ride into Bridger's Wells and are immediately struck by the fact that "after all the thinking we'd done about it, the place looked dead." Eyesight replaces thinking, establishing what will become the book's concern with using one's eyes to read people and situations. Gil and Canby, the saloon owner, then begin their ritual discussion of the painting that hangs behind the bar, and Monty Smith, the town drunk, moves in for his usual free drink. Like the animals of Mary Austin's *The Land of Little Rain*, Clark's people follow patterns that need to be played out. This need, together with the winter storings that demand release, place man in a physical environment that values the intellect less than the ability to respond to external stimuli. Thus Gil and Canby must work through their exchanges on the painting and the quality of Canby's liquor before they can begin to talk about more immediate events.

Given these needs, characters have varying degrees of skill in their ability to sense what is being asked of them by others. Many characters seem oblivious, responding simply to their own frustrations or desires. A few, like Canby, Davies, and Art, read a situation quite well and are able to maneuver others in order to avoid conflict. What is needed, therefore, is not a confrontation of ideas but a perceiver who can imaginatively "read" and integrate interacting selves within a physical environment—thus the importance of the appropriately named Art Croft.

Part 1 establishes the social context in which the narrative will operate and ends with the news that Kinkaid has been shot. It works within the controlled structure of the saloon presided over by the highly capable Canby. As one might expect of a bartender, Canby is good at reading his customers: "We kept on talking off our edge, Canby putting in a word now and then to keep us going." This statement suggests that Canby's effort to keep Art and Gil going has to do with his sense of their need to "talk off their edge." He's also good at understanding motives, as when he describes the women in Bridger's Wells driving Rose Mapen away because "they couldn't get over being afraid." The atmosphere within the saloon, as expressed in the various scenes of ritual, is one of energy on the edge of explosion, with the controlling bartender overseeing the action.

The complexity of part 1 results from this interaction of tension and ritual. Gil and Art are the only newcomers in a town where rustling has everyone suspicious. The poker game focuses on reading hands of cards, but the real subject is the effort and the failure of the men to read each other. When Farnley and Gil get into a fight, which is settled by Canby, Art details what in another narrative would seem largely irrelevant—the ways the two men regain consciousness: " 'He'll be all right,' I said. 'He always come out of it nice.' " Farnley, on the other hand, gives off warning signals: "Farnley was still out, but he was coming. His face was already beginning to swell, and his mouth was bleeding some from the corner. I didn't like the way he was coming back, slow, and without any chatter or struggle. Canby watched him too."

This description concentrates our attention not on what happens but on the subtle gestures that lead up to events. The poker game moves toward an inevitable fight because Gil and Farnley, in contrast to Art and Canby, fail to read the situation:

> I knew he wasn't cheating; Gil didn't. . . . But with his gripe on he wasn't taking his winning right. He wasn't showing any signs of being pleased, not boasting, or bulling the others along about how thin they'd have to live, the way you would in an ordinary game with a bunch of friends. He was just sitting there with a sullen dead-pan and raking in the pots slow and contemptuous, like he expected it. . . . But it was Farnley I was really worried about. He had a flaring kind of face, and he wasn't letting off steam in any way, not by a look or a word or a move, but staring a long time at his bad hands and then laying the cards down quietly. . . . I hoped Gil's luck would change enough to look rea-

sonable, but it didn't, so I dropped out of the game, saying he'd
had enough off me. I thought maybe he'd follow suit, but even
if he didn't, it would look better without his buddy in there. He
didn't, and he kept winning. I didn't want to get too far from
him, so I did the best I could and stood right behind him, where
I could see his hand, and nobody else's.

Typical of the action occurring in the saloon, the scene values perception, is highly sensitive to those forces which motivate or put an individual into motion, and establishes a complex of individual actions as
products of internal and external stimuli. Like a horse responding to a
nervous rider, the narrative responds to the smallest actions of these
individuals: "[Osgood's] voice was too enthusiastic and his manner
too intimate to be true, and while he kept strolling pompously among
the men, with one arm flexed behind him, the fist clenched, like the
statue of a great man in meditation, the other hand was constantly
and nervously toying with a seal on the heavy gold watch chain across
his vest." Like that of the poker game earlier, the description of this
scene focuses attention both on the gestures that express emotions
and on the perceiver sensitive to those gestures. Neither scene values intellectual knowledge. Even if Art *told* Gil, for example, what he
should not do, the knowledge would mean little without Gil's corresponding insight into the complexities of the moment.

In the context of a narrative in which people fail to read situations,
Canby's skill is clearly valuable but is restricted to the interior of the
saloon. Canby works well within the confines of his world. The story,
however, moves outside, where Art Croft and the reader become involved not only with men but also with animals and the environment.
Significantly, Canby does not join the hunt. He functions skillfully
within a particular context, but when the setting opens outward into
new territory, a new perceiver is needed. The situation outside differs
from that indoors. The plot moves to the hanging of Donald Martin
and his companions, but the book concerns itself with the breakdown
in vision that permits those deaths. In this, *The Ox-Bow Incident* presents us with circumstances that are the inverse of those in Mary Austin's *The Land of Little Rain*. Austin posits a world of integrating relationships; Clark posits a situation where men have refused or are unable to see relationships.[6]

Parts 1 and 2, with the setting of winter resolving into spring and the ritual acting out of stored aggressive energies, establish man's common bond with nature. The scenes of Gil and Art moving out of hibernation, the ritualistic move and countermove over the poker game, and the milling men outside Canby's saloon present a human world defined by the same urges that define thawing ground and anxious horses. A palpable sense of waiting characterizes the opening of *Ox-Bow*: the sheriff is out of town, and the judicial system is reduced to the comic. Previous systems, legal and judicial, have held groups of men together, but that time is passing—this is a border story. Rustling is on the increase, threatening both livelihood and, with the apparent murder of Kinkaid, lives. Something new is needed if the milling men are not to resort to anarchy. One alternative would reintroduce old systems—wait for the sheriff or get the judge. A second alternative, suggested by the figure of Canby in part 1, values the developing ability of the individual to "read" himself within his situation. Failure to do either results in the imposition of the most restrictive of systems, embodied in the southern-army background of Major Tetley.

Part 2 is a fine description of the effort to organize individuals of various persuasions into an effective force. Leaderless, the men mill about, looking for signs of direction. Horses sense the indecision; and both men and horses sense an approaching storm. "They'd be willing to quit if it was dark" indicates a physical rather than an intellectual response to the situation. Each individual watches others, trying to read shifting forces in order to sense direction: "[Ma] was greeted right and left when she joined us, and she spoke to Gil and me with the others, calling me 'boy' as she had when I'd stayed at her place, and we stood a lot better with the rest just on that." The real centers of action, little things, such as Ma's calling Art "boy," determine relationships, and so everyone watches carefully for words, gestures, or expressions that will indicate direction.

Many individual scenes could be used to demonstrate where the narrative action lies; that between Osgood and Smith is typical. Osgood, the ineffectual minister, wants the men to disband. Smith, the unpopular drunk, urges haste. When they speak, we witness a duel of which the outcome is both curious in itself and important for later group action:

The men stopped grinning. They didn't mind Smith joking
Sparks, but that offended their present sense of indecision and
secrecy. It seemed wrong to yell about a lynching. I felt it too,
that someone might be listening who shouldn't hear; and that in
spite of the fact that everybody in town knew.

Smith saw he'd made a mistake. . . .

The men laughed again, and Smith was emboldened.

"That is," he said loudly, "unless Mr. Osgood here is going
along. . . ."

"I'm not going, if it interests you. . . . I wash my hands. Will-
ful murderers are not company for a Christian."

That stung, but not usefully. A bawling out from a man like
Osgood doesn't sit well. Some of the men still grinned a little,
but the sour way.

"I was afraid the shepherd would feel his flock was a bit too
far astray for him to risk herding them this time," Smith la-
mented. Osgood was hit, and looked it.

The exchange indicates a struggle for power and the effort of the individual to define himself within the group.

The most outspoken individuals—Davies, Smith, Osgood—try out
their ideas directly with varying degrees of success. But in the above
exchange, little things rather than overarching ideas control action:
"And there's another thing I've noticed, that arguments sound a lot
different indoors and outdoors. There's a kind of insanity that comes
from being between walls and under a roof. You're too cooped up, and
don't get a chance to test ideas against the real size of things." The
control of part 1, occasioned by being inside Canby's saloon, finds its
usefulness weakened when set outside. Testing in the natural environment is essential, but the individuals of Bridger's Wells are not up
to it. With the sheriff away and the judge directionless, individuals
like Ma or Farnley or Davies have their moment, but the group finally
turns to Major Tetley.

"On the west edge of town he'd built a white, wooden mansion,
with pillars like a Southern plantation home, and big grounds around
it, fenced with white picket fence. The lawns were always cut . . . Tetley was like his house, quiet and fenced away." The embodiment of
enclosure, Major Tetley imposes his force on the group that has been
unable to give itself direction. The now organized posse/mob moves
out of town once more into a new setting, nature's high ground,

where in a blinding snowstorm life will depend upon the ability to read new conditions.

Part 3 moves the posse from Bridger's Wells to the Ox-Bow, with Art Croft playing a more conspicuous role than before. He has long talks with Gerald Tetley and Sparks and is wounded just beyond the center of the novel by a nervous stagecoach guard. After the shooting, Art serves increasingly as observer rather than participant; correspondingly, the problems of the novel intensify.

If we focus on a message in *The Ox-Bow Incident*, part 3 builds to the "point." When both Gerald and Sparks make their antilynching, antiposse views explicit, a point is clearly laid before the reader. In terms of this point the appearance of Rose and her husband makes sense. Rose's coming back to Bridger's Wells gives support to Canby's earlier statement about the jealousy of women in town. Rose is an attractive, dynamic, sexual force in an environment that apparently fears and drives away this energy. Within her newly found and socially acceptable role as wife, however, Rose can return to Bridger's Wells. The individual, in other words, cannot be permitted to flower outside accepted structures.

The men of Bridger's Wells are similarly unprepared to deal with the new figure of Donald Martin, the young man hung in part 4. Gerald Tetley is particularly bitter in making his point:

> "Men are no better," he said. "Men are worse. They're not so sly about their murder, but they don't have to be; they're stronger; they already have the upper hand of half the race, or they think so. They're bullies instead of sneaks, and that's worse. And they're just as careful to keep up their cheap male virtues, their strength, their courage, their good fellowship, to keep the pack from jumping them, as the women are to keep up their modesty and their hominess. They all lie about what they think, hide what they feel, to keep from looking queer to the pack."

The ideas of Gerald and Sparks, however, are less important as particular ideas than as examples of the increasing prominence of ideas. Ideas are not the only concern of part 3, but they begin to override Art's earlier narrative effort to pull together the violent individuals or to give direction to the milling mob. Parts 1 and 2 valued the need to read and organize. Part 3 places the need within a physical environment that threatens to inundate artificial constructs ("The road had been built up, like a railroad embankment, to keep it out of the spring flood") and to undercut Art's skills and commitment. As the men move along the trail, their talk reveals a variety of perspectives, from the isolation of Pete Snyder that "made me understand for the first time what we were really going to do" to the bitterness of Gerald, the grim experience of Sparks, and the morality of Davies. Art listens to these different positions while the horses struggle across the soggy turf, but he appears to lose interest in taking charge of his material. He initially tries to keep Gerald talking in order to maintain control over the hatred coming from him: " 'I didn't like the way the talk was getting to sound like a quarrel. I tried to ease it off.' " But he comes to reject Gerald as "babbling" on, a judgmental word, and finally moves away from young Tetley, stating that " 'I don't like to hear a man pouring out his insides without shame.' "

Perhaps Gerald's intense hatred should be rejected, but that same statement cannot be made about Art's next encounters. Gil, his winter companion, is upset by the possibility of a lynching, but, instead of playing an active role in their discussion, Art seems content to act as sounding board: " 'I don't like it,' Gil said. 'We can quit,' I reminded him. 'There's no law makes us be part of this posse.' " Instead of asserting initiative, Art simply reminds Gil that initiative could be taken and then talks him through his anger, more interested in reconciling quarrelsome differences than in shaping direction. In the physical gloom following this exchange, Sparks explains to Art that he, too, is disturbed by the posse's mission because, as a child, he had seen his brother lynched. Without any of the blind hatred within Gerald, Sparks is an entirely sympathetic individual, but Art is interested even less in listening to him than in listening to Gerald earlier. What particularly disturbs Art is the fact that Sparks, a black, doesn't address him as "Sir!" And he toys with Sparks's ideas: "When Sparks didn't say anything I felt I'd let another good man down, the way I had about Davies." Though sensitive to what each man says, Art appears more willing to compile information than to pull together differing fears and beliefs.

Lacking Art/"Art"—underscored by the accidental shooting of Art —the book moves swiftly toward its destructive conclusion. Part 3 pushes into the mountains and the snowstorm, where the ability to read men and situations becomes increasingly difficult, even though the riders seek to do just that. The sudden intrusion of the stagecoach appearing out of the gloom leads to a scene where milling men focus on discovering or asserting their relationship to the desirable Rose Mapen. Swanson, her husband, studies Gil while holding Rose's elbow "to show she was his property"; Gil, in love with Rose, studies Swanson while hooking his hands in his gun belt, "a bad sign." In addition, many of the men pretend that they see no weakness in Art after he has been shot, and Art makes clear his dislike of prying women. All of these gestures or comments stress once again that the action of the scene lies less in the events than in the understanding of events shrouded in gloom and confusion. " 'What are they [Rose and Swanson] doing up here at all?' " asks Gil. What the hell was the stage doing up here at night? asks Winder. What are all these men doing? ask the stage passengers.

When the men on the stage describe their passage through the Ox-Bow, inability to reconcile perceptions remains central: "Swanson and Carnes and Small had been telling Tetley about some men they'd seen, four, Carnes and Swanson thought, but Small thought three. . . . They had seen horses, but no cattle, but Swanson said the ravine was so black they couldn't have told past the fire." Whether or not the men were friendly, whether or not they were going to draw their guns, whether or not they were camped for the night—the driver and guard try to interpret, but they can't agree on what they have seen, much less on their interpretation.

In a context that denies reason's interpretive ability and that asserts the primacy of correctly reading circumstantial evidence, part 4 opens. "In a moment you couldn't tell which was riders and which trees." From the beginning, the book has played with the breakdown of individuals and structures while at the same time developing situations demanding clear vision. In part 4, with the representatives of the legal and judicial systems—the old systems—absent, lives depend on the integration of vision and thought. The narrative thus presses into a context where something new—whether leader, system, or insight—is demanded, for Donald Martin is a new force, an individual whose actions do not make sense. Reason, however, breaks down entirely, and three innocent men, Martin and his two companions, are hung.

The sheriff and judge return in part 5, where we might expect order to reassert itself, but their appearance only calls attention to their ineffectiveness. The judge rants about justice; the sheriff deals with the situation by claiming not to have seen anyone. Important at this moment is not the error of the mob/posse but the leadership that did not and does not exist. Nor is control reestablished: the narrative degenerates into a cacophony of noises and interpretations. Stories about what happened and why circulate through town, but no single narrative emerges. Art tires of listening to the rambling Davies, who tries to bring structure back into his story. Tetley and Gerald commit suicide, but their deaths hardly seem important as laughter rises from the saloon downstairs:

> Once, when he had subsided into the chair and was silent longer than usual, I could hear that Rose and her husband weren't down in the bar any longer, and after that I listened better.
> Even so it was hard talk to hear because there wasn't any answer. It was disordered and fragmentary . . . We couldn't bridge the gap; he was all inside, I was all outside.

Looking back to the opening of *The Ox-Bow Incident* from its closing, we must be struck by the deteriorating narrative structure. The opening flowed smoothly from the winter mountains into Canby's saloon and out into the streets of Bridger's Wells, as the interplay of human and natural forces sought organization. By the closing, nothing flows smoothly. Voices in laughter, confession, or speculation tumble over each other. The final words are given to Art's pleasure at getting out of town. The narrative begins with the living world's energies reasserting themselves as spring comes out of winter; it ends with death and noise. Forgotten are the early efforts of Canby and Art to make potentially explosive beings work together.

The Ox-Bow Incident vividly portrays new energies in a world of older, dying systems. It emphasizes the potential of the individual who can read and give direction to a textual situation wherein former systems of organization are absent or the circumstances demand new perceptions. The narrative values visual perception over intellectual logic, for the narrative operates in the high ground of new conditions; but without Art, without the perceiver, former systems take over, and chaos results. "We weren't a friendly gang anyway; no real friends in the lot." The internal coherence sought in parts 1 and 2 degenerates into mob violence; as the possibility of new relationships is lost, discordant interpretations become the dominant, final impression.

Several readers emphasize the prominence of the meadowlark in the opening and closing as symbolic of the book's implicitly hopeful message that with new knowledge, men will act better.[7] But this response, I think, imposes what readers want upon the actual experience of the narrative. One cannot deny that the meadowlark exists or that the story begins with spring coming out of winter, but these signs are less important in themselves than in their indication of the book's effort to move into new territory. Physically, the story moves toward mountainous high country; narratively, Art Croft tries to make a working unit out of disparate individuals. But both efforts break down and do so in such a way as to indicate the need for individuals who have the ability (and the courage) to look at a text and context without the blinders of inherited stereotypes.

7

The Conquest of Don Pedro:
Harvey Fergusson's "Long Rider"

Southwestern American writers have developed their own particular story of the land, one influenced equally by desert landscape and by an indigenous Mexican culture. The southwestern story thus blends the structures of a well-established society with an ironic recognition of their impermanence when set against the imposing and beautiful face of the land. The resulting fatalism, a sense of need or desire for structure connected with an awareness of inevitable passing, is at the same time strikingly communal. When traveling through this part of the country, one does not see the infrequent house that might signal the stereotyped loner or *isolato*. Instead, houses or trailers or shacks cluster together within the wide stretches of landscape. The people, in other words, have found that they need each other as much as they need the land.

A communal acceptance of struggle and inevitability as well as a sense of strength and beauty growing out of the natural setting characterizes Indian, Chicano, and Anglo-Saxon writing of the region. One of the area's most important writers is Harvey Fergusson, who was born in Albuquerque, New Mexico, in 1890. Fergusson's roots went several generations back into the settlement of the territory as well as to the East, where his father served as the first congressman from New Mexico. Fergusson remained fascinated with both directions, desiring ties to the East while developing an interest in the history of his land. Several of his most important narratives grow out of his interest in history: *The Blood of the Conquerors* (1921); *Wolf Song* (1927); *Grant of Kingdom* (1950); and *The Conquest of Don Pedro* (1954). *The Conquest of Don Pedro* has been variously described as a major piece of western writing, as the author's most important work, and as the finest novel to come out of the American Southwest.[1] However, it is also a text no longer in print, which indicates that book publishers view it as slight in commercial appeal. *The Conquest of Don Pedro* is nevertheless an impressive work, one that values the surfaces of the land and the lives seeking place on that land.

In contrast to the eastern narrative voice of individual disjunction, the narrative voice of such southwestern writers as Mary Austin, Raymond Otis, Frank Waters, and Harvey Fergusson is frequently third person, dispassionate, and objective. These voices pay attention not to idiosyncratic selves but to recurring patterns in the social world and the natural environment, patterns that value the continual forward motion of life. For example, *Wolf Song*, Fergusson's novel about Sam Lash and Lola Salazar, ends with the following: "Antagonists who could neither triumph, they struggled in a grip neither could break. . . ." Contrary to expectations, this is a description of two lovers, each of whom denies the independence of the other. The concluding ellipsis points indicate that the lovers' passionate conflict will reach beyond the immediate moment. In Fergusson, the sexual act—which he calls "the dance of dances"—presents a moment of intense struggle between two equal partners. Out of that intensity, life bursts forth; literal conquest, to the contrary, is destructive.

In its title, *The Conquest of Don Pedro* seems to point to the imposition of the eastern white male on a decaying society of Mexican heritage—the small town of Don Pedro conquered by the United States Cavalry and by the American free-enterprise system. However, a second consideration of the title raises the possibility that the act of conquest might be similar to the passionate embrace concluding *Wolf Song*, for the words could also imply that the town makes the conquest. Most accurate to the experience of the book would be to view Don Pedro as both conquerer and conquered.

The words *conquer* and *conquest*, together with such variations as *invade*, *challenge*, and *subdue*, appear frequently in this text and in contexts that indicate the struggle at the heart of the narrative is not one-sided:

> [Leo Mendes] sat down with his back to a wall, mopping sweat off his face with a red bandanna, surveying this place he proposed to *invade*. (emphasis added)

In truth the whole country had a quality of warm *submissiveness* about it. You might *struggle* mightily for a while but in time you were *conquered* by sunshine, silence and sleep. (emphasis added)

The Conquest of Don Pedro focuses, then, on the generative wrestling of two forces: the one is eastern, intellectual, commercial, and military; the other is southwestern and physical.

The Conquest of Don Pedro is the story of a town and a man, a Mexican town with a history "more a matter of legend than of record" and a Jew from New York with skills in commerce. The balance between old and new, the setting near the United States–Mexico border, and the post–Civil War time frame indicate that this novel falls within the tradition of western border stories. This particular border story, however, almost scrupulously avoids focusing on the border between man and nature, focusing instead on life within the town. That very avoidance, together with the particular events described, ironically direct attention to the individual and his relationship with the natural world, a relationship that enclosures cannot exclude. *The Conquest of Don Pedro* concerns itself with the discovery of that relationship.

The western border story, in particular the southwestern border story, is not one of the new crushing the old, of the invading white man taking over the town. When, for example, Frank Waters's *The Man Who Killed the Deer* (1942) moves to its conclusion, it emphasizes that, although the Navajo world is being subsumed by the world of the white man, both worlds must eventually pass; transition lies at the center of experience. The Indian in Waters understands transition, accepts it, and views it as engendering new life. The white man, however, rejects transition, valuing possession and permanence in order to expand his inherited European sense of limitation. Both Indian and white become part of a continued yielding to an ever-moving future:

> There can be no oases in the desert of ever-shifting time, no idyllic glades of primitive culture in the forest of mankind, no ivory towers of thought. We are all caught in the tide of perpetual change. These pueblos, these reservations must sometime pass away, and the red flow out into the engulfing white. The Government had only postponed the inevitable. [Byers's] resent-

ment gave way to a faint sadness. The victory, even for the Indians, seemed a shabby makeshift.

For it was predicted upon the differences between men, upon the outward forms of their lives, their ethnological behavior, and not upon the one eternally groping spirit of mankind. . . . So both must sometime pass: the Indian with his simple fundamental spiritual premise untranslated into modern terms, and finally the white with his monstrous materiality.

Like Waters, Fergusson uses particular individuals in particular moments in order to focus on that "groping spirit" within an environment of dynamic and fertile natural pattern.

In the Southwest, with its Mexican heritage and its striking landscape, transition is an important topic. Here, the imagination sees change as fundamental to ongoing processes that in turn provide strength and stability, even in a world constantly threatening to slip away. The Grand Canyon, for example, is continually being broken down by forces of erosion. Sheets of fractured rock, precariously balanced boulders, and fields of pebbles testify to the dynamics altering the face of the canyon, and these proofs of the unending forces of change take place within a framework of almost incomprehensible size and power. The very existence of the canyon—the thought of the energies that created it and the time frame within which they occurred, the marked delineations upon the rock escarpments that exhibit graphic evidence of the history of the planet—staggers the human imagination. When the Anasazi found shelter within the canyon's cliffs, they must have been as comforted by its strength as awed by its imperturbability.

Southwestern writing takes its characteristics from these interacting worlds which wrestle with change. With the exception of black literature, much traditional American writing stands horrified before those forces that threaten to destroy cultural values deemed of permanent worth. John Updike's stories focus on collapse; T. S. Eliot's poetry looks back to the hope of traditional roots; Edward Albee's plays rip away illusion. In Thomas Pynchon or John Barth, the future seems predicated upon the individual being able to come to terms with a world of artifice.

Much of the shock in eastern writing stems from what earlier Americans usually reveled in—their lack of a usable past.[2] The melting pot was supposed to turn a disparate and dispossessed band of refugees into a hardy new breed of men and women whose vision was fixed on the future; that was the dream, but the twentieth-century individual struggles with the discovery that, after his plunge into the melting pot, he, like Nathaniel Hawthorne's Hepzibah Pyncheon, has lost his roots. Without connection to soil or heritage, modern man is—as Woody Allen portrays in *Zelig*—less Adam than alien.

Anglo-Saxon southwesterners have certainly experienced the "horror of the melting pot," having left both Europe and eastern America. Their roots do not run as deep as the Chicanos' or the Indians'; the result is a certain flatness in their character and writing. Offsetting rootlessness, however, is the omnipresent land. Though an individual's sense of himself does not emerge in relation to class or ancestor, it does emerge in relation to physical place and to those who share that place with him. The narrative of the Southwest therefore has much to offer a twentieth-century American society of Walter Zeligs and Harry Angstroms.

Like his earlier novels *Wolf Song* and *Grant of Kingdom*, Fergusson's *The Conquest of Don Pedro* is a story of individuals who erect and attack enclosures within a world of powerful forces. Enclosures play a prominent role in all of Fergusson's works. Both physical enclosures (the "crumbling ruin of a great house" in the beginning of *Grant of Kingdom*) and cultural enclosures (the framework of Mexican society that attempts to shut out the protagonists in each book) offer resistance to the sweeping rush of sexual passion and shelter from the enormous spaces dwarfing individual lives. Men and women in Fergusson attempt to fortify themselves against forces that continually move them out of their enclosures. Individuals seeking a balance between resistance and participation form the basis for struggle in the novels:

> Just as before, it was his weakness that softened her. After all, she had won. . . .
> He touched her at first as though she had been of dangerous substance but when his hands felt her unresisting warmth he lost his fear. He crushed her in his arms, and her face, backflung to meet his mouth, was a mask of willing pain.

Antagonists who could neither triumph, they struggled in a
grip neither could break. . . . (*Wolf Song*)

The protagonist of *The Conquest of Don Pedro*, however, is made uncomfortable by such generative antagonism. Early in chapter 2, "Coming home late one night Leo saw a soldier and a Mexican girl grappling
on the ground in the dark plaza, and the guttural fury of their desire
left him shaken and disturbed. The place seemed overcharged with
youth and energy, with passions engendered by the sudden conjunction of two races, erupting into lust and battle, as though conqueror
and conquered struggled violently to become one." Disturbed by such
grappling, Leo Mendes does not fulfill the traditional role of a conqueror. Intellectually, Leo plans a successful commercial assault on
the little Mexican town, but, physically and emotionally, he finds himself drawn into the lives of the people. He plans a victory but becomes
victor and victim. We therefore have a story of an individual who
places himself in the center of social and biological rhythms that then
overwhelm his carefully defined intentions.

Appropriate to the overwhelming nature of these rhythms, *The Conquest of Don Pedro* is intensely sexual, with much of the power generated by the narrative's restraint. The narrative voice speaks in the past
tense, maintains an objective distance from its subject, and almost
studiously avoids evocative language or syntax:

> The town of Don Pedro stood on the eastern edge of the lower
> Rio Grande Valley, where it spreads out more than a mile wide
> and the silver river loops and wanders through the lush green of
> growing crops and the bosques of cottonwood, willow and over-
> grown mesquite. Although its history was more a matter of leg-
> end than of record, Don Pedro was known to be a very old town.
> When Leo Mendes came there shortly after the Civil War it must
> have been at least two hundred years old.

These opening words to the text appear to contradict my statement
about past tense ("spreads") and distance ("loops and wanders
through the lush green"), but the opening sentence juxtaposes past
tense ("stood") and present tense ("spreads")—human activity is in
the past; natural movement is in the present. That relationship diminishes the significance of individual initiative, placing it within a physically rich and flowing environment. Even in this brief opening paragraph, the rather flat verb *to be* is used five times, contrasting

markedly with the earlier "loops and wanders." *To be* remains prominent throughout the text, diminishing activity and passion in the verbal structures. In moments of antagonism, however, as in the scene witnessed by Leo and quoted above, *to be* disappears.

The restraint exercised by the narrative voice urges recognition of the voice's centrality and of its effort at control. Given the passionate content of the narrative, the voice remains strangely dispassionate, seems to struggle against the content—inactive and past-tense verbs, unexcited syntax. Additionally, little effort is given to making characters visually striking, and dialogue, which lets us hear directly a character's words and which offers a way into his thoughts, plays a minor role in the text. In contrast, the earlier *Wolf Song* spends considerably more time with dialogue and with descriptions of people and places: "Up from the edge of the prairie and over the range rode three. Their buckskin was black with blood and shiny from much wiping of greasy knives and nearly all the fringes had been cut off their pants for thongs. Hair hung thick and dirty to their shoulders. Traps rattled in rucksacks behind their Spanish saddles and across the pommel each carried a long Hawkins rifle of shining brass-bound steel and battered wooden stock." The detail in this, the opening, and other passages in *Wolf Song* results in a book more visually oriented than *The Conquest of Don Pedro*. Leo and his world remain difficult to see even after repeated readings; the use of the past tense, the neutral *to be*, and the striking prominence of the calm narrative voice result in a text that forces the reader to observe action rather than become swept up in it.

Similarly, the text's structure reflects a control like that evidenced in the language. There are fourteen chapters of varying numbers of sections and pages (see table 1). This structural pattern gives the reader an experience of control and increasing speed. Leo Mendes moves into his new life in Don Pedro with careful deliberation, but the skill demanded of him is less intellectual than adaptive—the ability and willingness to respond to situations as they arise, and they arise with increasing rapidity. Neither deliberation nor responsiveness can shield Leo from the startling energies working in the sleepy, Mexican border town.

Table 1. The Structure of Harvey Fergusson's *The Conquest of Don Pedro*

Chapter	No. of Sections	No. of Pages
1	7	34
2	12	44
3	6	18
4	4	22
5	5	20
6	4	15
7	3	17
8	5	15
9	5	17
10	4	17
11	1	6
12	2	9
13	2	6
14	2	5

As the chapters progress, the number of sections and pages in each decreases, mirroring the situations rapidly getting out of Leo's control. The only chapter in which Leo maintains a dominant stance is the first, beginning with his planned invasion and concluding with his emerging new store and its "defiant sign ['LEO MENDES: Tienca Barata'], a challenge to the old and established powers and customs." But even this initial control is conditioned moments before by the brief appearance of Lupe Vierra: "She was so close he could smell the perfume she wore, mingled with a vague odor of feminine presence. He felt a stir of desire toward her, and also of antagonism . . . She left Leo feeling slightly shaken."

The second and longest chapter presents a flashback that further questions the control implied in the opening. Driven out of New York by his failing lungs, Leo accepts with both pleasure and reluctance his new opportunities in the Southwest. "Leo was properly afraid of Apaches and bandits, but he had the self-assurance of a man who has carefully considered the facts." The Mexicans, however, "made him learn to dance just as they made him learn to swim," and the girls become a "growing problem." When he is selected by Dolores Pino, Leo's assurance begins to slip: "It seemed to him now that he had become only the carrier of his seed, that his only object and errand in life was to go to this woman and pour himself into her."

Leo does not choose Dolores, Lupe, or Magdalena; they choose him, making his intellectual/commercial intentions subject to their procreative force, which needs him as much as he discovers he needs it: "Leo was aware also that [Dolores] had quickened his destiny." Leo rapidly becomes less an initiator than one who takes advantage of the energies presented to him by women. Forced to leave the ways and people he had come to love, just as he was forced to leave those he had loved in New York, Leo moves at the end of the second chapter to begin his assault on Don Pedro.

The opening two chapters, the longest in the book, thus establish a deliberate, eastern, commercial mind caught up in forces that move him. The first half of the book, by page count, comes in the middle of chapter 5, where Leo is at the height of his conquest. He has been welcomed by the town, has had a long sexual relationship with Lupe Vierra, and has finally seen Don Augustin Vierra come to him to borrow money. By chapter count, however, the middle of the book does not come until the appearance of Robert Coppinger, who will be responsible for Leo's eventual departure from Don Pedro. Structurally, therefore, as the increasing brevity of the chapters reflects forces that move Leo, the double middle undercuts any illusion of conquest. Leo is at the height of his material victory in chapter 5, but the appearance of Robert just before Leo's marriage to Magdalena indicates that dividing the book between chapters 7 and 8 is a necessary counterpoint to dividing it in the middle of chapter 5.

Control is sought by the intellectual powers at the top of the social structure in order to protect against the natural world's "wide open spaces," which civilizations (and Leo Mendes) fear. But the natural world keeps breaking through. In spite of what my emphasis on control may cause its first-time reader to expect, this is not a dull or dispassionate narrative; particular individuals and moments—Leo Mendes, for example, or the poker games of Don Vierra—are set against and within larger forces which sweep language and individuals into their ongoing movement: "Then suddenly one night Lupe began to talk, and once she had started talking words poured from her mouth in eager profusion. She never talked when she had her clothes on, and she never said a word until her ardours were over, but lying naked and peaceful she at last achieved something of self-revelation." The passions and the stripping away of clothes consume and then release language and self-revelation. Like Lupe, the narrative voice seems to be operating after the boilings of passion. Deliberately controlled words pour forth as though seeking to understand the "dance of dances" between two cultural antagonists at a pivotal moment in history.

Against this carefully constructed frame, tone, and syntax, a story of change plays itself out. The male in Fergusson embodies the forces of intellectual and commercial change, but the procreative female challenges the male's intentions and provides for movement in accordance with the unvarying rhythms of nature. In chapter 4,

> He rode home in the cool of the small hours wondering what if anything Lupe intended. He sensed a touch of cruelty in the woman and of hatred for men in general. Something of that he had felt in a good many Mexican women, who were all treated by their husbands and fathers as articles of property primarily. They had no rights and no freedom but what they stole. In general, they seemed to accept this as the divine order, but with an underlying resentment, and in Lupe the spirit of protest and rebellion was armed with a sharp mind and a restless spirit. Very likely she took pleasure in disturbing his peace of mind and keeping him bewildered and probably that was the only triumph she sought.

The explosive moments in this book result from the tension between the controlled narrative voice or the Mexican social structure and those flashes of "restless spirit" that violate even the most deliberate of intentions.

The dispassionate background serves to enhance the hints of passion: "Moreover, in her typical, restless way she contrived to toss her pretty slender legs about so that she seemed to be constantly on the verge of an intimate revelation." Lupe, Leo, Don Augustin, and Padre Orlando Malandrini are seated in conversation at the Vierra house when this description is given. "Repeatedly [Leo] found himself seated opposite her, often a little too far away for ready conversation, but always in such a position that he could contemplate her with ease, and in fact could not avoid doing so." Leo's distance from Lupe, the presence of her husband and Padre, the patriarchal structure that houses them combine to give Lupe's gestures their special excitement. Her distance together with her invitation present a challenge, but Leo does not like this kind of challenge, this "very slight intercourse . . . a wordless communion in which she adorned and revealed herself for his eyes." This challenge "would be bad for business and also hard on his peace of mind"; "no man ever wanted trouble less," and, "after all, here he was the invader." Later, at a dance, he becomes "aware that she had been building up a desire in him for months, slowly and artfully, and that this was the final hard thrust of her attack, the challenge that could not be mistaken."

These events, separated by days or weeks, appear together in chapter 4, section 2, one of the two longest units in the book. The other—chapter 10, section 4—details Leo's discovery that his wife Magdalena is having an affair with Robert Coppinger. Length in both instances creates unrelieved tension, which contrasts with the typically briefer sections and the consequent detachment that keep the reader from spending too much time on any single moment. Lupe's attack concludes at the dance: "Her dancing had the same elusive coquetry as all her other gestures, and gave him the same feeling of provoked frustration. It did, that is, until just before the music stopped, when suddenly she bent in the middle and thrust herself against him so that just for a moment their legs were tangled and their bellies were tensely intimate." This scene unites Leo as "invader" and Lupe as the attacker who flashes a "dramatic command" to which he must respond. The moment presents Leo and Lupe as antagonists and serves as prelude to the "dance of dances."

In their formal control and explosive passion, both dances—the musical and the sexual—express structures similar to those used by the narrative voice in constructing the text. In John Ford's movies—*My Darling Clementine* and *Fort Apache*, for example—highly stylized dances express a perceived need for the imposition of order in the violent west. In the movies of Sam Peckinpah—*Ride the High Country* and *The Wild Bunch*—dance is explosive with passion. Harvey Fergusson integrates both the order and the passion, the effort to maintain control yielding to an energy that takes over and brings forth new life.

After Leo learns that Magdalena, his wife, has been involved in a sexual love affair with Robert Coppinger, the Texas horse dealer and Leo's friend, numerous statements place Leo in the role of narrator: "He was more the author of Magdalena's character and feeling than anyone else." In addition, he tries to use words to control feelings and struggles to see his situation clearly, thereby finding discipline and becoming a force in making destinies. But Leo's authorial role, like that of the dons in the history of the little town, is quickly subsumed within the passionate forces, which go on creating life. Those forces overwhelm both the narrator's textual control and Leo's desire to author Magdalena. Discipline as a narrative act is necessary but of only limited value in the world of Don Pedro; what is required is an individual responsive both to his own strengths and to the demands of his environment, ultimately allowing authored creations to find their own life.

The night Leo leaves Don Pedro for the last time, his friend Padre Malandrini speaks of discipline: " 'I feel sure Magdalena needs this man [Coppinger]. She has always remained a child in her relation to you. Now she will have to grow up. And so will he. I believe he has been just a youth bent on adventure, not bad but wild. Now he has found a discipline and I am sure he knows it.' " Discipline needs to grow out of the wildness. Leo's authoring of Magdalena imposed structure on her energy; with Robert, Malandrini says, form will emerge from their maturing relationship and the social/natural environment of which they are a part. Leo's experience in Don Pedro has been similar: "For the first time in his life, [Leo] was glad of wilderness, of space and solitude." A city-bred New Yorker, Leo had always been frightened and had escaped space by seeking the everyday details of busy human existence. But that kind of struggle now takes its necessary place within the larger context of physical space. "He knew it was foolish to waste the strength of his horse and soon he settled down to the easy jog, which is the standard gait of long riders all over the West." Finding the standard gait of the long rider, discovering the pace that allows movement but does not break man or horse, is the story of Leo Mendes.

In both the narrator's stance toward his narrative and the material chosen by the narrator, *The Conquest of Don Pedro* focuses on the need of the individual to find his place as a particular within a world of

dynamic forces, to become a long rider. Leo interests the narrator because Leo is a man from the East whose background emphasizes
his comfort with enclosures—"Always his life was one of crowds and
walls and noises in a swarming human world, an enclosed world of
people pressed together in mutual dependence." Leo is, therefore, a
figure who will appreciate the church (Padre Malandrini is also from
New York) and the structures of Mexican society. As a Jew, Leo is a
wanderer who values the past. He is also something of an intellectual,
one who plans his assaults. In addition to these characteristics, however, is the fact that Leo likes beginnings: "Leo came of a race of reluctant pilgrims, of people who loved family life and security and
peace and yet had traveled halfway around the world, always in flight
from something or in search of something. This was a conflict that ran
in the blood, and Leo knew that it ran in his own, for there was something in him that loved the road and something that longed for a
home." Leo combines a fascination with change and a commitment to
the traditional; in him, therefore, lies the potential of the individual to
work toward an integration of the personal desire to secure a piece of
ground and of the breadth of vision to realize the transitory nature of
that endeavor.

> [Leo and Lupe] were creatures of different kinds and born of dif-
> ferent worlds and would never think or feel alike, but lying na-
> ked in dark and quiet they had left all worlds behind, had
> crawled back into the womb of their common humanity, telling
> each other in muted voices about their so different lives, while
> crickets make a small nearby courting music and a faraway dog
> howled his feelings at the moon. (chap. 4)

> When he had stripped and mounted [Dolores] she made a con-
> tinuous guttural sound deep in her throat. It seemed to have in
> it nothing of her usual voice or of any human voice but to be a
> subhuman music of desire, of the pure and innocent lust that is
> common to man and beast. (chap. 2)

Leo's is the discovery of common human bonds and common animal
lusts. The discovery of those interconnections within and between society and nature makes possible Leo's transition from a solitary individual who cherishes his own powers to an individual who realizes
that his selection by Dolores and Lupe demands that he not fail the
biological forces driving for regeneration. Finally, as a "long rider,"

Leo moves toward becoming an individual who can combine personal power with insight into his place within an evolving universe. That interaction between the desire to secure and the thrust of the dynamic describes the structure, plot, imagery, and syntax of *The Conquest of Don Pedro*. The sweeping forward of the text, the lusty energies, the particular individuals, the narrative voice, the structures erected by transiting individuals—all are central to the discovery that space and the rhythms of a natural world are more demanding than the desire to enclose and seek protection from change.

8

Wright Morris: Living in the World

Poststructuralist criticism responds to the modernist sense of alienation by rejecting the assumption of essential individuality. Replacing the belief in essences has been the assertion of codes and texts with and within which man operates. From that perspective, the effort of Ernest Hemingway or Harvey Fergusson to place the individual within a world of creative force is both invalid and naive.

However, as I have argued, not all American imaginations operate on the basis of eastern assumptions. In the West and the Midwest, where land and life in a physical world are central, individuals seek to align the patterns of their lives to complement the patterns within the environment. To Wright Morris (1910–), one of the most productive contemporary writers, realignment is what the narrative imagination always seeks to do: "Each time the writer creates and solves the problems of fiction, he makes it possible for men and women to live in the world."[1] Breaking through artificial, enclosing constructs and establishing contact with the energy of living processes is the story of western and midwestern writers. This effort initially has to struggle with frustration, which can become despair, or with nostalgic longing, which can produce stasis.[2]

"If we should ask ourselves," says the Nebraska-born Morris in *The Territory Ahead* (1978), "what it is that the common and the uncommon American have in common, the man in the street and the sophisticate, the hillbilly and the Ivy Leaguer, I think we have an answer. Nostalgia. . . . Stock taking, inventory, is the first effort of the mind to make itself at home."[3] When Clyde Muncy, the protagonist and narrator of Morris's *The Home Place* (1948), moves his family from their apartment in New York City to his boyhood home outside Lone Tree, Nebraska, both nostalgia and desire for freedom motivate him. " 'There is no grass in New York,' says Clyde, 'no yards, no trees, no lawn swings—

and for thousands of kids not very much sky. They live in cages. . . . It's like a big zoo of kids. A cage with windows and bars.' " During the course of his story, Clyde discovers the obvious, that you can't go home again; but his act of return initiates the process of "stock taking" that enables him to abandon nostalgia.

Clyde Muncy's problems are reflected in the divided narrative that is *The Home Place*, in this case a divided narrative with unusual divisions. On one side of a page is Clyde's first-person verbal narrative; on the facing page is a series of photographs with their own story. At numerous points, the two texts interrelate, but the division between the verbal and visual worlds mirrors a division in Clyde between his head and his eyes. That division stymies Clyde's impulse to move. He is stuck in nostalgia somewhere between New York and Lone Tree, the urban and the rural, the verbal and the visual. "Each time the writer creates and solves the problems of fiction, he makes it possible for men and women to live in the world." *The Home Place* presents us with an obvious fictional problem in the separation of image and word; the effort to solve that "problem" so that men and women can "live in the world" is both the story of Clyde Muncy and that of the Wright Morris canon.

The photographs in *The Home Place* are black-and-white stills, which have the effect of freezing a fluid world of color into isolated artifacts.[4] The pictures lack human life (we see the human face, for example, only through photographs of photographs), are high-definition close-ups, and stress man-made vertical or horizontal lines. A drab angularity in the pictures emphasizes the fact that natural and human life are missing. Because of the interest in close-ups, we also lack context. We are presented with pieces and made to speculate about the environment in which those pieces exist(ed).

The use of vertical and horizontal lines imposed on natural backgrounds—a fence post driven into barren ground, for example—calls attention to the human forces that broke the Nebraska ground and built the farms and town. These forces countered those in the natural world which would have driven away most people. The lives are therefore testaments to strength; but the unbending quality of the verticals and horizontals testifies both to a stubbornness and to a pride that led to the great dust bowls and a world now lacking color and life.

Given the effect of the pictures, one begins to see a division between what Clyde Muncy wants to find in his return to the home place—a world where his kids can learn to live—and the actual place to which he is returning. There is remarkably little sky in the photographs, for example, and it was sky that Clyde particularly missed in the cages of New York City. We begin with a story that was motivated by nostalgia but that quickly discovers the discrepancy between that impulse and the reality of "home."

But there is more to this story. As the viewer lives with the photographs, something else begins to happen. Even though no human and remarkably little natural life exists in the pictures, they do not image a dead world. There is "life" here, the felt lives of the people who built the fences, slept in the bed, wrote the poems, or sat in the barber's chair. Though not a life one can return to or recapture, it is real all the same. The discovery of that life coincides with Clyde's discovery of life where he least expected it. When he and his wife, Peggy, visit a neighboring house, he wonders, "What is it that strikes you about a vacant house? I suppose it has something to do with the fact that any house that's been lived in, any room that's been slept in, is not vacant any more. From that point on it's forever occupied. With the people in the house you tend to forget that. . . . But with the people gone, you know the place is inhabited." The empty spot on a wall where a calendar used to hang or the old caning in a new chair establishes what Clyde comes to see as "connections" between his world and the life no longer visibly present. When Clyde makes that connection, he is ready to leave the home place, for he has taken stock of his own life.

We do not know where Clyde Muncy goes after he leaves Lone Tree, but we can watch Wright Morris work to solve "the problems of fiction" in the books that follow *The Home Place*. Indeed, Morris's effort is to integrate the verbal and the visual, to put life into motion, and to draw on energy inherent in the natural world.

In Orbit (1967) is a particularly appropriate text to compare with *The Home Place* because *In Orbit* also centers on a picture. This picture, however, is significantly different from the pictures in the earlier book: "That's the picture. You might want to add a few details of your own," says the narrator after the initial description of his protagonist, Jubal E. Gainer. Later, in the last pages of the text, the narrator comments, "That's the picture: there are those who can take it in at a glance. . . .

But perhaps the important detail escapes you. He is in motion." The picture referred to, the totality of events described, results from a narrative fusion of verbal and visual, and the dynamic quality of the picture is evidenced in its use of line. The photographs in *The Home Place* emphasize horizontals and verticals, but the opening of *In Orbit* develops a different kind of line: "This boy comes riding with his arms high and wide, his head dipped low, his ass light in the saddle, as if about to be shot into orbit from a forked sling. . . . He is like a diver just before he hits the water, he is like a Moslem prayer-borne toward Mecca, he is like a cowpoke hanging to the steer's horns." The verticals and horizontals of *The Home Place* imply the possibility of a vector, but the resultant is missing. With no directed force, we simply have two lines and consequent freezing of motion. *In Orbit*, however, presents a story of force and motion; the picture taken in at a glance is that of the vector itself, the integration of vertical and horizontal forces. Because the subject moves, the details and forces continually change, and the narrative eye capable of perceiving and articulating this dynamic picture must be able to integrate, whereas the earlier vision was limited to fragmented freezing.

The contentment with nostalgia, which generated the fragmentation of *The Home Place*, is ultimately life denying. No human faces are seen in the photographs, and there is only indirect evidence in either the verbal or the visual text of the energy originally embodied in the pioneers. We see the products, not the process, of the settlement that established new life on the prairies. In contrast, energy is the subject of *In Orbit*. In spite of its dispassionate surface, *In Orbit* is a highly sexual book. A divided imagination denies the possibility of new life, but an imagination that seeks to take in a fluid, thrusting world appropriately sees a story that is destructive of the static condition of verticals and horizontals (here portrayed in the cutting of the old oak tree) and at the same time explosively creative. When the joyfully named Jubal E. Gainer enters Pickett, "the words of his song string out behind him like the tail of a kite" or like the tail of a comet or the tail of a twister or perhaps even the tail of a sperm cell. "As for the overall impression of the boy on the bike, it is that of two cats, piggyback: hard at it." Twister or sperm cell, the thrusting force embodied in Jubal Gainer is creative because it explodes internal energies and brings new energy to the individuals in Pickett, Indiana. Nature abhors a vacuum, we are told, and the natural forces of Jubal and twister rush into the vacuum at the center of the town and its inhabitants, as imaged in the frequently mentioned phonograph record. When that center lies within an individual, the energy stimulates life as a sperm cell drives toward an ovum.

Little distinguishes Jubal from other teenagers; the narrator in fact makes every effort to stress Jubal's ordinary characteristics. No knight-errant conscious of his direction and in control of his intentions, Jubal has the sniffles.[5] But Jubal's special quality is not his physical appearance or his intellectual prowess; it is rather the fact that he operates out of the center of himself. Characters in the book accuse him of intention, but Jubal functions naturally, responding directly to stimuli of the moment. Like human sexual relations, his relations with others are center to center, in contrast to the relationships established by the inhabitants of Pickett, where impersonal, distancing newspapers and telephones unite the citizens. Jubal almost instantaneously establishes physical, interpersonal contact with his "victims." He seldom speaks, so the contact is not verbal, nor does he impose himself on others. Jubal is welcomed by his victims, who similarly respond from within themselves.

These implicitly sexual center-to-center relationships occur in a fertile environment awaiting penetration. Two of the most pervasive images, bees and spray, establish an atmosphere of fertility. The events of *In Orbit* occur on May 17, a spring day in Indiana. Warm, overpowering smells of springtime fill the air. Bees swarm in the cloying, pollen-laden atmosphere, their masculine activity mirrored by frequent scenes of spraying: Pauline Bergdahl hoses down cinders, a plane sprays for insects, and two Pickett firemen hose the sidewalk. Unlike the bees, however, each of these human actions consciously seeks to hold back natural forces, which might imperil the smooth functioning of an ordered society. The spraying also connotes ejaculation. "Because he is non-fixed, this one also sprays the fireplace and the white sidewalls of Alan's Porsche." That description of one of Charlotte Hatfield's cats makes clear the connection between sexuality, fixing, and spraying. The book's dispassionate surface reflects the suppressed sexuality of Pickett, but underneath are individuals and a natural world ripe for fertilization. Jubal's victims are beings of potential, and his energies either deflate or stimulate what is within. Energy is transferred, as in an electron's jump from one orbit to another, so that when Jubal leaves Pickett "there is no longer much flex in his knees, much spring in his legs. The words of a song do not trail out behind him like the tail of a kite." His potency has been spent and needs time to regenerate.

Given the book's interest in both motion and sexuality—to be alive is to move—the frequent uses of the word *fix* are entirely correct. To fix is both to pin down and to remove sexual potency. Holly Stroymeyer "is a gentle, childlike woman, and like a child she loves to wander. . . . It's the wandering that had led to problems." And Charlotte Hatfield does not have "much sense of place. . . . Charlotte has been trained to live in a house, to use her box, and to purr when petted. But like the cat in her lap, she is a creature who has not been fixed." In contrast to the sexually stimulating and fertile women, the men in Pickett are unwilling or unable to become sexually aggressive: Haffner is "more AC than DC"; Alan Hatfield can "place the needle in the groove" but doesn't seem to excite Charlotte; and Sanford Avery is limited to rubbing his crotch at the *idea* of sex.

The central male figure, other than Jubal, is Curt Hodler, a newspaper editor with possibilities, but an individual who works best in a fixed world: "But the forecast is less important than the date, May 17th. The date, strange to say, is more important in the long run than anything in the paper. Day in and day out the news is pretty much the same. . . . It is the date that gives it meaning. . . . If the paper loses its dateline it loses its mind. The purpose of the forecast is to pin down the day, whether it rains or not." Like Stephen Crane's correspondent or Sherwood Anderson's George Willard, Hodler and his occupation indicate his possibilities and his limitations. A man of words in a book whose narrator is keenly sensitive to language, Hodler prefers to fix meaning to words and to stories. He suppresses his potential just as he suppresses his sexual desire for Miss Holly. His envy of Jubal is the envy of action:

> "And how is Miss Holly?"
> For more than twenty years Avery's cynical answer had been the same. *Who the hell would know that?* Now thanks to some snooping idler, or passing stranger, that was no longer an idle question. Someone finally knew. It is a torment to Hodler that this essential knowledge is what he once desired for himself.

How *was* Miss Holly. Some idle lecher, some wandering pervert, some bored delinquent, some loyal friend or guardian, envied but unknown to Hodler, and still at large, finally knew.

Pickett's dealer in army/navy surplus, Kashperl, also prefers to fix events, although he, too, is fascinated with action. "Is it more than a tree that falls? It falls to give this day its meaning. To give Kashperl a cud for his idle, vagrant thoughts." For Kashperl, meaning is something tangible to cling to in a day when experience appears chaotic. "A preference for the fading title, or the missing author, or better yet the rare volume that proved to lack both, a country waiting to be staked out and mapped by Kashperl," indicates both Kashperl's potential—he deals with the "clothes of men *missing in action*"—and his preference for fixing the unknown. He is content with being sedentary, with vicariously living off the experience of others. Both Hodler and Kashperl find an event food for thought rather than stimulus to action. Kashperl even shares the desire of Avery and Hodler for Miss Holly: "But that was not what the fat man was waiting to hear. He wanted what Jubal had had without all the trouble. He wanted the cherry."

Structurally, Jubal's encounter with Kashperl—chapter 5—is at the center of the nine-chapter book; in chapter 5 Jubal is also at the physical center of Pickett. He penetrates the town just as he does individuals, revealing a fertile world ripe for stimulation. The bag of cherries smashed on Haffner's head nicely images the condition of the town and Jubal's effect upon it: Kashperl—and Hodler and Avery—"wanted the cherry, which was actually more than Jubal had got." The earlier book, *The Home Place*, breaks in two, a verbal and a visual text; *In Orbit*, however, is a single picture, initially taken in at a glance and then probed. Instead of a two- or three-part structure, *In Orbit* is a verbal/visual whole that seems to be continually moving. It is very difficult, for example, to speak of its beginning, middle, and end. Instead, we move into and then out from Pickett and its inhabitants. Chapters 1 and 9 present the picture taken in; chapters 2 and 8 focus on the force that is Jubal; chapters 3 and 4 (Holly) and chapters 6 and 7 (Charlotte) narrate Jubal's stimulation of two sexually responsive women; and chapter 5 presents the bloodless puncturing of the town's center. The movement of the book is suggestive of the sexual act itself, a penetration that breaks cherries, shatters hollow dreams, and is followed by withdrawal.[6]

In Orbit, then, is a picture of a single motion; our effort as viewer or reader is to see the whole rather than to extract meaning. The picture combines the deceptively simple and apparently static with the powerfully dynamic. Clyde Muncy's vision of the world in *The Home Place* was dominated by division and meaning, but the narrator of *In Orbit*, as evidenced by the picture he describes, sees a world of motion and unity. His use of language in that description is part of the vision:

> This boy comes riding with his arms high and wide, his head dipped low, his ass tight in the saddle, as if about to be shot into orbit from a forked sling. He wears a white crash helmet, a plastic visor of the color they tint car windshields, half-boots with stirrup heels, a black horsehide jacket with zippers, levis so tight in the crotch the zipper of the fly is often snagged with hair. Wind puffs his sleeves, plucks the strings of his arms, fills the back of his jacket like a wineskin, ripples the soot-smeared portrait of J. S. Bach on his chest. His face is black as the bottomside of a stove lid, except for his nose, which is pewter-colored. He has the sniffles and often gives it a buff with his sleeve. He is like a diver just before he hits the water, he is like a Moslem prayer-borne toward Mecca, or he is like a cowpoke hanging to the steer's horns, or a highschool dropout fleeing the draft.

The use of detail and figurative language, particularly striking in this passage, characterizes much of the writing in the book. The narrator approaches language as though it were at the same time a visual and a verbal medium. Curt Hodler, the newspaperman, struggles to perceive shape, while the narrator enjoys exploring the motion of an integrated picture. Like the narrative and the structure, the language is an act of penetration—thus the fascination with metaphor and simile. In contrast to Hodler, who needs to use language to fix change, the narrator is sensitive to the power of language to open, focus, extend, and expand our perceptions. For the narrator, language is not a device to get at meaning. *In Orbit* yields very little "meaning"; rather, it describes an event. The verbal medium penetrates, probes, that event. The lines that conclude the paragraph quoted above take the crisply detailed opening and put it into motion by allowing the imagination the freedom to work with those details. Thus the opening lines both particularize—"This boy"—and set in motion the picture that will continue to be explored. The narrator perceives a world of possibility, and his ability to use language allows him to penetrate, experience, and verbalize that world.

In an essay entitled "The Immediate Present," from a book of critical essays, *The Territory Ahead*, Wright Morris discusses what he sees as the relationship between art and life. "We have a need, however illusive, for a life that is more real than life. It lies in the imagination. Fiction would seem to be the way it is processed into reality. . . . If man is nature self-conscious, as we have reason to believe, art is his expanding universe." The fiction of Morris is a particularly good place to see the expanding universe of one man's imagination. The urge is to live fully in a universe whole and alive. *In Orbit*, then, is only in part the story of Jubal E. Gainer. It is also part of Morris's imaginative attempt to explore the territory ahead, to conceive and articulate an integrated, dynamic, fertile—in a word, a living—image.

9

Valuing Surface:
The Imagination of Ivan Doig

Among westerners, the appearance of *This House of Sky* in 1978 led to interest in and respect for a new writer, Ivan Doig. Among easterners, however, Doig continues to be largely unknown. Ivan Doig was born in 1939 in White Sulphur Springs, Montana, and grew up along the Rocky Mountain front, where several of his books take place. After establishing a career as a free-lance writer, he settled in Seattle, Washington. Doig's growing reputation in the West and his relative obscurity on the East Coast suggest, I believe, that his work embodies the qualities I have been detailing and challenges the assumptions of contemporary criticism, which do not perceive surface as having essential substance. While Doig shares with his fellow westerners a concern for the direction of society, he is a writer who does not lament current conditions; instead, he pursues "place" within his particular physical and social environment.

In a talk given at the 1987 meeting of the Western Literature Association, Harold Simonson suggested that "place" need not be restricted to an interest in regional writing or a horizontal focus on geography. Vertically, said Simonson, a sense of place makes the individual aware of where he stands within and what he shares with ecological and social systems. I have shown how among western writers Lewis Garrard begins the search for place and how this search continues in the work of such writers as Mary Austin, Ernest Hemingway, Wright Morris, and Harvey Fergusson. Ivan Doig brings that search up to the present, making it the core of his imaginative work.

Readers familiar with Doig would expect any discussion of his writing to begin with *This House of Sky*, the book that brought him significant attention and a nomination for the National Book Award. However, Doig's first published book was *News: A Consumer's Guide*, cowritten with his wife Carol in 1972 and important because it reveals much about relationships that develop later in Doig's imagination. *News* represents a cautious first step, one taken together with his wife. More significantly, the co-writing hints of the function of family in Ivan Doig's work and in western literature generally.

Family is not a subject that generates much interest in the scholarship of the traditional American canon, unless one is talking about the deteriorating familial structures in such writers as Hawthorne and Faulkner. The traditional central figures—Leatherstocking, Ishmael, Huck Finn, Isabel Archer, Carrie Meeber—move away from family. Midwestern and western writers, however, give prominence to family: Hamlin Garland, Willa Cather, Conrad Richter, Frank Waters, and Wallace Stegner come to mind, as do such ethnic writers as Rudolfo Anaya, Leslie Silko, and Scott Momaday. Like the ocean in Stephen Crane's "The Open Boat," western space in its enormity demands human interaction. From the pages of James Pike's tale of his harrowing experience with blizzards to the opening scenes in Hamlin Garland's *Boy Life on the Prairie* emerge pictures of individuals acutely conscious of themselves in relation to the physical environment. Under conditions in which surface and place are central, human relationships become crucial.[1]

Valuing surface focuses attention on discrete events and on the ability of the individual to respond to those events. The title of *News: A Consumer's Guide* seems therefore especially appropriate to the imagination's effort to understand surface, pointing both to the discrete events designated "news" and to the fact that these events are important less in themselves than in the response of individuals to them. Interesting, of course, is that Ivan Doig, an individual who has chosen to spend his life working with the verbal packages called "words," begins his career with an examination of how these packages are made, how they relate to the physical world, and how they are consumed. "A word is like a section of telephone cable," says Doig, "a sheath with several conduits inside it. Each of the conduits can carry a different meaning, but all within the same unit." "News stories are made, not born. Made by workers and machines that refine random happenings into bundles of information."[2]

When Doig discusses the editing of news, he talks about the consumer's act as well as the more traditional role of the newspaper or television editor—interpretation being the common denominator in both instances. Selecting material to be reported is certainly an important step in the process of receiving news, but the consumer's perceiving act provides the distinctive focus of Doig's book. Because the narrators in all Doig's work function as consumers seeking to understand and facilitate the perceiving act, we should expect that in his books Doig will not jump from event to event but will work with events themselves.

Given his interest in event, it is not surprising to see how Doig chooses to focus his next and best-known work, *This House of Sky*. *News* indicated that only with consciousness of the event's shaping could an individual make use of (consume) that event. With *This House of Sky* Doig turns to the event that is himself and begins a process of particularizing that will extend to his next book, *Winter Brothers*. From the general (news and consumer) to the particular (*this* house), Doig begins to apply ideas developed in the relative safety of impersonal moments to the more crucial concern of an individual life, and, for Doig, such definition is intensely verbal.

"Where [my father's] outline touched the air, my knowing must truly begin." The narrator returns to this image at the end of the narrative: "My single outline meets the time-swept air that knew theirs." "Outline" in each case points to the narrator's perception of the centrality of surface; each outline establishes a point of contact with other surfaces. The word *outline* also has clear verbal connotations appropriate to an imagination that, in the previous book, has established its sensitivity to language. "That is as much as can be eked out—landscape, settlers' patterns on it, the family fate within the pattern— about the past my father came out of. I *read* into it all I can, *plot* out likelihoods and chase after blood hunches. But still the *story* draws itself away from the dry twinings of map work and bloodlines, and into the boundaries of my father's own body and brain" (emphasis added). "Story" is important to Doig because events in his landscape function within a developing narrative; becoming aware of his life within that story requires that he train his visual and verbal skills.

Like that of Scott Momaday's *House Made of Dawn*, the title of the narrative, *This House of Sky: Landscapes of a Western Mind*, points to a perception of structure and enclosure significantly different from that developed in the East, where the architectural metaphors of Henry

James dominate the literary landscape. With Doig and Momaday, as with Austin and Hemingway, structure depends upon a physical organic environment. These are "Landscapes of a Western Mind," not the narratives of the Great Plains or the adventures of a Montana sheepherder. "House," "sky," "landscapes," "western," and "mind" integrate to form an image of an imagination seeking its place within a world dominated by land and sky. The interrelating of physical and mental landscapes define the focus of the narrative.

"I glance higher for some hint of the weather," says the narrator at the end of the second section, "and the square of air broadens and broadens to become the blue expanse over Montana rangeland, so vast and vaulting that it rears, from the foundation-line of the plains horizon, to form the walls and roof of all of life's experience that my younger self could imagine, a single great house of sky." Tony Tanner has said, extending the argument of Richard Poirier's *A World Else-where*, that when the American builds his house of style, he withdraws into it, seeking a "stay against diffusion." Alexis de Tocqueville made a similar point 130 years earlier: the American "shuts himself up tightly within himself and insists upon judging the world from there."[3] Taken together, these statements present a picture of the traditional American imagination as cut off from and unable to relate to the world. Ivan Doig's "house," in contrast, is something that one expands into, that allows the individual to embrace rather than exclude. Doig's house is thus the inevitable outcome of the difference between the protective imagination of Francis Parkman and the inclusive joy of Lewis Garrard.

The opening and closing lines of Doig's narrative define the shape of the book:

> Soon before daybreak on my sixth birthday, my mother's breathing wheezed more raggedly than ever, then quieted. And then stopped.
> The remembering begins out of that new silence. Through the time since, I reach back along my father's tellings and around the urgings which would have me face about and forget, to feel into these oldest shadows for the first sudden edge of it all.

> Then my father and my grandmother go, together, back elsewhere in memory, and I am left to think through the fortune of all we experienced together. And of how, now, my single outline meets the time-swept air that knew theirs.

The narrative springs out of "new silence." Learning to speak within that silence, getting from the opening to the closing lines, is an effort that necessitates seeing the self within the context of family and environment. In the first sentence, the sixth birthday and the mother's dying breaths go together—youth and age, child and parent, health and illness, beginning and end—not as distinct from each other in separate sentences but as interrelated within one sentence. *This House of Sky* does not dwell on the mother or, more particularly, her death. Its focus moves quickly out of death in the direction of expanding life. In fact, the first seven words imply eager, youthful anticipation. The strikingly abrupt first paragraph does not initiate a narrative of a young person breaking free from confinement but of a narrative voice—and one distinctly older than six years—moving immediately into the second paragraph, where its effort will be to "reach" and "feel" back along its father's tellings in spite of "urgings" to forget.

Those tellings call attention to both the communal and the individual acts of narration, acts that permit outlines to meet within the common story. Replacing the chronological continuity of chapters, seven sections develop a continuity growing out of the narrator's acts of remembering; the first section, the brief "Time Since," establishes memory and language as the prominent concerns of the book. The last two pages of the first section discuss memory as "a set of sagas we live by. . . . That such rememberings take place in a single cave of brain . . . makes them sagas no less." This particular saga, this "thirty-year story," begins in "Time Since" with the narrator working to capture something of his mother, something that eludes him—particularly because he does not have the sound of her voice, "the one thing which would pulse her alive for me." He has other voices, though, voices that appear in italics and talk about her. And he has black-and-white photographs—"I coax from the photos . . . as if I might finger through the emulsion patterns to the moments themselves"—striking in their detail of the moment and frustrating in their lack of the life that was his mother.

Most important, the narrator has his own voice, one that creates images and uses language to detail the surfaces that once were the life of the early surroundings: "The single sound is hidden water—the south fork of Sixteenmile Creek diving down its willow-masked gulch. The stream flees north through this secret and peopleless land until, under the fir-dark flanks of Hatfield Mountain, a bow of meadow makes the riffled water curl wide to the west." One of the great pleasures in reading Ivan Doig is the discovery of a language that seems to want to touch the world's surfaces. The more one reads of Doig, the stronger the sense that Doig uses language as a vital point of contact between the individual and the natural or social worlds.

Mary Austin's *Land of Little Rain* contrasted the fluidity of Indian naming with the effort of the white man to fix change by imposing single, definitive names. The Indian recognized change in the surface, the outline, but he also recognized substance in the essence of the individual. Doig's perception is much like that of the Indian, with an additional white man's sensitivity to the desire for resisting change, for succumbing to the "urgings" to forget. Consequently, the technical devices throughout Doig's writings—the alliteration and assonance in the passage above or the gradually shifting accents in *Dancing at the Rascal Fair*—are ways into "place" rather than means of escape from the vagaries of life: "That is as much as can be eked out . . . about the past my father came out of." Language for Doig is a prominent means of "eking" out.

So also does Doig's imagery integrate imagination and natural environment; in the following sentence, language and imagery combine to sustain the imagination as the wind sustains the hawk: "Alone here on our abrupt time shelf, the three of us eased through May and the first twenty-six days of June secure as hawks with wind under our wings." But this idyllic world within the Bridger Range of southwestern Montana, cut off from the outside except for the weekly delivery of supplies, cannot itself be sustained; it ends with the death of the mother—"the clockless mountain summers were over for my father." The two males are forced to seek the nurturing of place rather than that of wife and mother. "I coax from the photos" begins the imaginative and narrative acts of consuming events, acts outlined in *News: A Consumer's Guide* and that now become the driving force of *This House of Sky*.

This House of Sky is a story not of breaking free but of discovering and accepting "place," defined early in the text as the name given to any "piece of land where some worn-out family had lost eventually to weather or market prices." As in Wright Morris's *The Home Place*, these locales are in reality less geographical than human, their substance very real even if not tangible. "One such place was where our own lives were compassed from," with "compass" suggesting the inextricable bond between individual and land, what Morris speaks of as "making connections." Narratively, Doig's text compasses from such "places," detailing with an eye for surface and outline the patterns that reveal lives and relationships. "Little by little, and across more time than I want to count, I have come to see where our lives fit then into the valley."

Some of Doig's narrative compassing is achieved intellectually, as when he speculates about "place" or memory or when he outlines such past events as the arrival of his ancestors in Montana, but the compassing achieved imaginatively, the effort verbally to bring surfaces of the past into contact with experiences of the present becomes increasingly distinctive of Doig's writing.

> Before we could reach the corral, a sharp rain began to sting down. The mountains had vanished, and the gray which blotted them already was taking the ridgeline. Chill sifted into the air as the rain drilled through. Now a wind steadily sharpening the storm's attack. The sheep milled in the corral as if being stirred by a giant paddle, quickening and quickening. A stalled wave of them had begun to pack so tightly against the wooden gate that Dad and I together couldn't undo the wire that held it closed; the gate bowed, snapped apart against the tonnage of the hundreds of struggling bodies. . . . And so we fought, running, raging, hurling the dogs and ourselves at the waves of sheep, flogging with the gunny sacks we had grabbed off a corral post, shaking the wire rings of cans to a din, and steadily as the rain shot down on us, we lost ground. We were like skirmishers against a running army. We might bend the band slightly and gradually toward the coulee, but all the while their circling panic was carrying towards the cliffs now not more than a few thousand yards away. Only several minutes away for sheep running headlong. It was not yet midday, and grayness had clamped in on the ridgeline over us as if to rain for the rest of time.

Even a long passage such as this one cannot adequately suggest Doig's careful attention to detail. In scene after scene, the narrative reaches for the substance of the moment via the focus on detail. The particularity can seem like nothing more than a showing off of verbal skills—and perhaps that is the central problem a writer like Doig must continually confront—but what Doig seeks is consciousness of the moment. He seeks detail not for its own sake but for the sake of verbal contact with the detail.

Like the forest fire in *English Creek* and the blizzard in *Dancing at the Rascal Fair*, the battle described above does not lend itself to symbolic reading, nor does much of Doig's writing. He is not writing a history, trying to get his facts correct; nor is he trying to transcend the physical world through the symbol. Instead, Doig's world has solidity, as conveyed in the passage above by verbs that appeal to the senses—the "rain began to sting down"—and by descriptions that make nature an active, physical force—the gray "blotted" (instead of the more clichéd expression, "blotted out") the mountains. Varying sentence structures and lengths—one sentence incomplete; one sentence nicely balanced against the semicolon like the sheep against the gate so that the sentence itself seems to bow as the gate does—reinforce the portrayal of two men struggling. Scenes such as these indicate the effort of imaginative coaxing, the eking out of the substance of events, which will allow outlines (that of the event and that of the working imagination) to touch.

Part of that imagination's grappling with the past is its recognition of the need to struggle forward: "If there was any mooring in our lives now, it was my schooling." Education, which in an earlier sense meant a leading out, becomes a central topic as Doig leaves Montana for school in Chicago in the second half of the book. This traditional leading out—this move *East*—does not produce the freedom hoped for; in fact, the section detailing that move, "Ivory," is the choppiest in the book. We are given letters and fragments of activity rather than the extended descriptions of events that characterize the other sections. The schooling, the mooring, is accepted by all as valuable, but the particular form of the mooring, a doctorate and the study of journalism, does not lead to the expected results; the narrator has not discovered the desired skills for coaxing life from outlines. The previous section, "North," concludes:

> The words of all the ties of blood interest me, for they seem never quite deft enough, not entirely bold and guiled enough, to speak the mysterious strengths of lineage. . . . What I miss in our special blood-words is a sense of recasting themselves for each generation, each fresh situation of kindredness. It seems somehow too meager that they should merely exist, plain pack-

ets of sound like any other, and not hold power to texture each new conformation with the bright exact ones that are yearned for. . . . For my father had to be more than is coded in the standard six-letter sound of "father."

In the final section, "Endings," the father is dying, the being "who enchanted into me such a love of language and story that it has become my lifework." Consuming, integrating that connection into himself therefore becomes essential to the narrator and provides the stimulus to the text.

The book, then, is shaped by the dying of the parents and the consequent imaginative growth of the child. Out of the frustration with the loss of the physically fertile mother and with the narrative effort to break through the verbal code of "father," Doig comes to value the land and people and to see the need for verbalizing that value. "All of his way of life that I had sought escape from—the grinding routine of ranching, the existence at the mercy of mauling weather, the endless starting-over from one calamity or another—was passing with him, and while I still wanted my distance from such a gauntlet, I found that I did not want my knowing of it to go from me. . . . I had begun to see that it counted for much." Seeing requires speaking if outlines are to touch, but speaking requires an internal education, and intellectual growth alone will not do: "Exactly at the point of my life when I had meant to turn myself to teaching, to the routined assurances of scholariness, I found myself veering inward instead."

The inward veering eventually produces *This House of Sky* and the struggle of "my single outline" to meet "the time-swept air that knew theirs." This action might generate little more than sentimentality were it to remain an expression of homesickness, but the looking into the narrator's past, his contact with the father, generates new movement and a new story, just as the focus on *News* generated the interest in the event that was himself. The narrative voice once again moves, in *Winter Brothers* turning to the historical past and its relationship to the historical present.

All of Doig's writings to date depend on a collecting and consumption of data, the act of a natural creature functioning at the peak of its ability within the natural world. In *This House of Sky*, the imagination wrestles with voices, facts about ancestors, photos, and personal experience in an effort to understand itself in relation to the lives closest to it. In *Winter Brothers*, the imagination moves temporally, going back one hundred years to the life and writings of James Gilchrist Swan, a man who occupied geographical spaces similar to the narrator's own. The effort is to discover narratively a brother, an individual with whom the narrator shares space, motivation, and values: "Here is the winter that will be the season of Swan. Rather, of Swan and me and those constant diaries. Day by day, a logbook of what is uppermost in any of the three of us. It is a venture that I have mulled these past years of my becoming less headlong and more aware that I dwell in a community of time as well as of people." As in *News* and *This House of Sky*, the narrator begins by combing data, studying pieces of paper (containing some 2.5 million handwritten words), trying to put a life together, his own and that of a figure who, in "Day Sixty," is "doubly valuable to me because the people of my own blood are gone now, buried in Montana, the storytellers, reciters of sayings . . . and Swan is an entrancing winterer—a tale-bringer, emissary from the time of the first people."

Once again, it is the effort of outlines to touch, here temporally rather than spatially, that motivates *Winter Brothers*. Doig reads Swan and watches Doig read Swan, and he focuses on the outline of events every bit as intently as he focused on news events in his first book:

> He scares me a little, though, about this winter's effort at precision, my try at knowing as much as possible of Swan. There is that easy deceit of acquaintanceship. . . . If I myself am such an example of private code, how findable can Swan be in his fifteen thousand days of Diary words? Findable enough, I still believe, for by now I have a strengthening sense of how it is that some of those coastal paths which for so many years carried him now hold me. But Swan does maintain boundaries, often numerical ones, with that deft pen. He may let me know exactly what size coat he wore, yet generally is going to make me guess about the inside of his head. Which perhaps is as much as one measurer can comfortably grant another. ("Day Twenty-Five")

Data is what all of us have to work with. A postmodernist would stress the limitations, the sufficiency of the codes; in Doig's writings, working with codes allows contact with other outlines.

Winter Brothers begins slowly, almost formally, as the narrator sets out on what seems a relatively easy intellectual endeavor, one that ought to work—he will gather some information from Swan's writings and "lop it into magazine-article length." However, the relationships between the two—no, three—lives, particularly the relationships between the writings of Swan and those of the narrator, begin to interrelate: "No question: the stickum that holds his life together is in his inkwell," perhaps most accurately the inkwell of the imagination. Both men are westerners, meaning for Doig that each tries to push his imagination to the coast, the limit of its capability—"I wonder whether something more is not urging him as well: a longing to step away, if only temporarily, to a new horizon. To the next West he can find." That westeringness fascinates Doig, an individual excited even by tracking rodent prints in the snow. It is the tracking that counts, even if tracking leads to the discovery that "the edge of America can also be a brink."

This intellectually confident but imaginatively tentative opening does not characterize the book as a whole. At first glance, both *This House of Sky* and *Winter Brothers* appear to be intellectually clever, somewhat self-indulgent commentaries on time, space, and surface, but that is not an accurate assessment of either book. Each demands the reader's careful attention and moves quickly away from an intellectual struggle with pieces of data. The father and the land emerge at the end of *This House of Sky* in a way that no selective quoting can detail. *Winter Brothers* begins as a study of the past but ends as an integration of outlines: the Indian Haidas " 'weren't bound by the silly feeling that it's impossible for two figures to occupy the same space at the same time.' " The book places Doig's story within Swan's; Swan's life provides the structure of the divisions of the text, while the narrator's developing insight into relationship influences the organization of material within the divisions. What begins as a curious parallel/disjunction between two westerners becomes finally the junction of two imaginations:

> Swan did not write those words. I have written them for him, or rather, for both of us, this dusk of winter and of his life. . . . From that eighty-second birthday of his, where my imagination takes over the telling, he has four months and a week to live.
>
> But I discover an odd thing as this companion of my winter begins to fade from life. There at the first days of this century Swan comes into view to me in a strong new way . . . Swan stepping to the century-line which I crossed in his direction almost three months ago now has endured into time which

touches my own. . . . Unlearnable, those beneath-the-skin frontiers. Even the outer ones leave questions, for I believe now that no one winterbook—no book—can find nearly all that should be said of the West, the Wests. . . . What I do take from this time of musing in Swan's Wests is fresh realization that my own westernness is going to have to be a direction of the mind.

Swan's carving of a swan on the cliffs overlooking the sea punctuates this winter narrative, is a stone dot "that puts period—the seed of ellipsis [spoken of earlier as compressed through shorthand into the period] for whatever continuation is on its way—to this winter."

In these three books, the imagination of Ivan Doig builds on the efforts of the westerners of the imagination who preceded him, picking up Lewis Garrard's energy, Mary Austin's attention to the physical world, and Wright Morris's perception of the centrality of relationships. With *The Sea Runners*, Doig turns in a new direction but continues his commitment to event and surface. *The Sea Runners* again focuses on a moment in the past, but not with Doig as conscious presence; talking about Swan's life is replaced by detailing the lives of men who escaped from a Russian camp and made their way down America's West Coast. In *English Creek* and *Dancing at the Rascal Fair*, Doig begins a trilogy that recreates the lives of the ancestral Scotsmen who settled Montana. Once again the narrator explores the event that is his own world but now attempts to touch its surface without intellectualizing the process. As always, Ivan Doig takes narrative chances. In *Dancing at the Rascal Fair*, the narrator, Angus McCaskill, enjoys life's rhythms; he wants to see, says his lover, Anna Ramsay, "how many ways life can rhyme." The narrative he produces is one of those efforts at dancing with life, but in Doig that means dancing with storms both of the country and of the heart while keeping your wits about you through flood, blizzard, drought, and desire.

Doig's writing, from *News: A Consumer's Guide* to *Dancing at the Rascal Fair*, is a sustained imaginative work struggling to put into motion the surfaces that might otherwise overwhelm. In Wright Morris's terms, "each time the writer creates and solves the problems of fiction, he makes it possible for men and women to live in the world," and so Ivan Doig has done in finding a place for the individual.

10

After Words: The Western Movies of John Ford and Sam Peckinpah

The western story plays a particularly important role within the context of the American imagination, for the western story explores and communicates the strengths and responsibilities of human life within social and physical ecosystems. Consciousness of surfaces leads to consciousness of rhythms common to the individual and to his environment, opening the way for new relationships and a new story.

Readers of canonical contemporary American literature are all too aware of its tormented voices, voices that reflect a loss of the sense of place. Because distrusting place leads to overweening ego, a sense of superiority within an ecosystem, and isolation, opening the canon to western as well as ethnic and feminist perspectives offers a significant corrective to the perspective of modern alienation.

Throughout my discussion I have focused on prose fiction, arguing that works accepted into the traditional literary canon have in common a preoccupation with enclosure based upon discomfort with the openness of space. This imagination finds the energy of the physical environment stimulating, but it is convinced that without the human commitment to enclosing and reshaping the natural, stimulation too often produces anarchy. This imagination therefore works within physical (houses, forts) or social (class structure) or cultural (myth) enclosures. In contrast, another aspect of the American imagination seeks to realign itself with the openness of space.

Narrative, of course, is not limited to prose fiction. The implications of my argument extend beyond the literary to the visual and practical arts and even to politics and foreign policy, where enclosed image has long had a troubling centrality. I will focus here on the visual arts, in particular on the western movies of two of America's most prominent directors, John Ford and Sam Peckinpah, whose work evidences the contrasting responses to the demands of space. Ford, an easterner by familial and cultural background, is attracted to but strongly distrusts space; his movies argue for the advantages of enclosure despite the unfortunate loss of energy it causes. Peckinpah, a westerner who is an outsider when judged by establishment values, loves to work with the challenges of open land. Each man narrates a particular story of change; together, their work demonstrates the diversity of the American imagination.

John Ford's vision of the West is quintessentially traditional.[1] He sees the West as simultaneously harsh and magnificent. The Monument Valley setting used in so many of his westerns is undeniably beautiful, but its beauty is most appreciated from a distance. Up close, the landscape threatens to swallow or violate the individual or group. Consequently, the setting of a Ford movie makes humanity and civilization appear highly vulnerable.[2] The beauty of the West must therefore always be placed within frameworks that offer protection to the white man and his values—I emphasize "the white man" because Ford's movies see the Indian as an element of the threatening land. When Indian vulnerability appears, it results from eastern interference. Ford's primary concern is civilization as the white man knows it.[3]

Consequent upon the concern for civilized values is the fact that Ford's western movies are highly protective of young white women— Dallas (*Stagecoach*), Clementine Carter (*My Darling Clementine*), Philadelphia Thursday (*Fort Apache*), Olivia (*She Wore a Yellow Ribbon*), and Debbie Edwards (*The Searchers*), to mention a few. The casting of these roles emphasizes female vulnerability. Cathy Downs, Shirley Temple, and Natalie Wood all have delicate features that image fragility. Even when more visually aggressive women are cast—Joanne Dru and Maureen O'Hara, for example—their carriage and costumes indicate that they, like Cathy Downs and Shirley Temple, embody the refinements of civilization.

A Ford western therefore has much in common with James Fenimore Cooper's *The Last of the Mohicans* in that both feature the movement of young women into the interior of the wilderness. Their presence necessitates army troops and sheltering forts, but Cooper explodes his shelters, casting individual family members into the wilderness. Ford never portrays that kind of story—the struggles of the one female forced to live in the wilderness, Debbie Edwards in *The Searchers*, are not part of the movie. In Ford, threatening wilderness is held in check by representatives of society and by communities that strengthen as they pull together. Though Ford's doubts about the complete goodness of civilization are suggested in several places—for example, in *The Man Who Shot Liberty Valance* (1962)—such doubts are always subordinated to maintaining traditional values.

Stagecoach (1939) began John Ford's love affair with a carefully constructed image of the West. If we keep in mind the dusty, crumbling stagecoach that figures prominently in *Liberty Valance*, the earlier movie begins a story that concludes in *Liberty Valance* with Hallie Stoddard noting that the wilderness has finally been turned into a garden. However, there is no visual garden in 1939 or, for that matter, in 1962. The title of *Stagecoach* points to what the movie is all about, focusing our attention on the tiny, fragile enclosure carrying individuals of distinct social classes through a barren, threatening landscape. Even worse, the Indian inhabitants of that landsape have broken loose and begun to destroy. Appropriate to Ford's values, the one image of Indian destruction is a burning enclosure and a dead, very young, and very pretty woman.

The enclosure that is the stagecoach is pulled (it has no power to move itself) through the threatening landscape by numerous teams of horses guided by the capable but exceedingly nervous hands of Buck. Andy Devine plays Buck, and Devine will reappear in *Liberty Valance* as the town marshal of Shinbone, where he is incapable of maintaining law and order. The casting of the bumbling Devine as the driver in *Stagecoach* reinforces the image of vulnerability as the coach tries to work its way to the suggestively named town of Lordsburg. *Stagecoach* carries viewer and passenger from one physical construct to another, and most of its story takes place in a town or stage stop or the stagecoach itself. A relatively small amount of emphasis is given to the camera looking at the surroundings. Wilderness, in other words, is more a brooding concern than a reality in this movie, a technique that increases the terror associated with the physical world.

Ultimately, of course, neither Buck nor the stagecoach can protect the individuals inside. In an important and highly effective scene late in the movie, the camera pulls back to show the tiny stage racing across flats so barren that they might have been filmed on the moon. Savages chase behind, and clearly it is only a matter of moments before they will catch the fleeing stage. When all the little society's ammunition has been used on the Indians, destruction seems inevitable. But out of nowhere appears the cavalry, civilization's official protective arm on the frontier. The Indians are routed and the stage brought safely to Lordsburg, where the second concern of the movie, cruelty among men, is reconciled. Dallas and Ringo depart in the final scene to marry and settle down on Ringo's ranch.

Stagecoach presents us with a political as well as a social statement about the need of individual members of society to work together and draw upon the forces of law and order to defeat natural savagery inherent in any wilderness condition. After all, 1939 was the year savagery was threatening what Europe and America stood for, and it is not surprising that Ford was then concerned with the relationship of enclosure and wilderness. That he sets his concern in the ominous landscape of Monument Valley says a great deal about his perception of the West as a place to test and hone the values of civilization.

The implications established in *Stagecoach* are carried forward and explored in Ford's later westerns, all of which appear after World War II.[4] The title of *My Darling Clementine* (1946) and the music that accompanies the opening credits once again emphasize the vulnerability of the woman, a figure who, as the song says, is lost and gone forever. In several of his movies, Ford relies heavily on opening music to establish an upbeat tone that will prove dominant in spite of wilderness threats; the particular songs played, "My Darling Clementine," "Jeanie with the Light Brown Hair," and "She Wore a Yellow Ribbon," all praise the joys (and loss) of young womanhood.

Even though she will not appear until almost halfway through the movie, Clementine Carter is central to *My Darling Clementine* because of the values she brings to Tombstone, Arizona. Shortly after Wyatt Earp enters the town in the movie's opening minutes, he asks a question that is often repeated: "What kind of a town is this?" That question, and Clementine Carter, are what the movie is all about. *Stagecoach* visualized the dangers inherent in trusting oneself outside of the town construct. Once Ringo kills Hank Plummer, the town of Lordsburg is presumably safe for families. *My Darling Clementine* brings us

out of the wilderness (as the movie opens) and into the town of Tombstone, where families are not safe; it then confronts the nature of civilized societies. At the end, when the town has been made safe for
young people such as Clementine, Wyatt Earp rides on.

Given the centrality of Clementine Carter, the threat posed by the
Clantons (a family without women) is not possible confrontation with
the Earps but harm to the traditional values of family and culture.
The movie's setting emphasizes the fragile nature of the town within the enormity of surrounding wilderness, but physical wilderness is
of minor concern. Earp's question—"What kind of a town is this?"—
asks about human wilderness and the need for culture (Shakespeare),
women (Clementine), churches, and effective law enforcement.
Against those forces, the Clantons are doomed, and we know all along
that they are doomed—given the fact that the story of the Clanton-
Earp shoot-out at the OK Corral is so great a part of western mythology. The Clantons are largely a brooding off-camera presence. The
tone of the opening "My Darling Clementine," the seriousness with
which Granville Thorndyke delivers Hamlet's soliloquy, and the placing of church and communal celebration at the center of the movie
combine to make us believe in these values rather than worry about
the Clantons. Having no fears about Wyatt and his brothers emerging
victorious, we can enjoy the focus on the civilizing process.

After *My Darling Clementine*, Ford's story moves back into the wilderness, and the cavalry becomes the center of attention rather than
the *deus ex machina* it was in *Stagecoach*. Though towns and presumably
western civilization after World War II have been made safer, moving
the subject of the movies to the communal life within wilderness forts
suggests that western society continues to need vigilance and protection. Even the figures of Hank Plummer, Old Man Clanton, and
Doc Holliday from the earlier movies indicated that the internal problems of white society itself are ultimately greater threats than the external savages. With *Fort Apache* (1948), *She Wore a Yellow Ribbon* (1949),
and *Rio Grande* (1950), the same holds true. The movies again value
women and family, as evidenced by such songs as "There's No Place
like Home" and "I'll Take You Home Again, Kathleen."

The cavalry in *Stagecoach* arrived at the last moment to destroy savagery and to protect women and a newborn baby. *Fort Apache* opens
with another stagecoach, which brings the new cavalry commander,

Lieutenant Colonel Owen Thursday, and his daughter into the wilderness. Thursday curses the land, while his daughter (Shirley Temple)
plays with his frustration and clearly enjoys the prospects of their new
life. We do not open, in other words, with an externally threatened
stagecoach and a timid female protected by soldiers. The appropriately named young lady from the East, Philadelphia, is in fact so in
command of herself and the young men who surround her that she
never seems threatened. Moreover, though the Indians commit terri-
ble acts, the movie asks us to share their shame and outrage when
Thursday humiliates them and treats them as a people without honor.
We continue, therefore, to see society as a vulnerable construct set
within a threatening environment, but the fort is much more protected than the earlier stagecoach. The commander of the fort and his
strengths and weaknesses are the objects of focus; the threat to Fort
Apache is primarily internal.

As the cavalry trilogy develops, the internal problem intensifies
through two new elements in the Ford story. *She Wore a Yellow Ribbon*
spends a great deal of time outside the fort, and Ford filmed the movie
not just in color but in spectacular postcard color. The commander of
the cavalry, Captain Nathan Brittles (played by John Wayne), is aging,
and possible future commanders, such as Lieutenant Flint Cohill,
seem too young for the task. The two new elements in the Ford story
are therefore the almost unreal visual beauty of the physical wilderness and the image of loss prominent in the human story. When Captain Brittles saves both Indian and white from battle by driving away
the Indians' horses, no one is hurt. We are left at the movie's end to
worry more about the abilities of young Olivia and Flint Cohill than
about a wilderness that has been visually highlighted more for its
beauty than for its danger.

In 1956, loss becomes the entire subject of the appropriately entitled
The Searchers. *Stagecoach* and *My Darling Clementine* asserted the need
to build defensive personal and social structures in order to protect
vulnerable values. In the cavalry trilogy, that theme was maintained
but overshadowed by a sense of internal loss. The title of the 1956
movie makes it clear that loss is now real and search the central concern. The object of the search is embodied in the figure of the young
girl, Debbie Edwards. Ethan Edwards, her uncle (played by John
Wayne), searches for her accompanied by a young man of mixed

blood, Martin Pawley. Ethan is retired from the southern army, a man who does not believe in surrender and who has lost to his brother the woman he loved, Mary Edwards. Throughout the movie, Ethan's driving passion is hatred, particularly hatred for savages.

Like *Yellow Ribbon*, *The Searchers* is filmed in almost extravagant color. When combined with Ethan's hatred of Indians, the intense color suggests something self-destructive working within the movie, for we are presented simultaneously with extremes of the land's beauty and with the central figure's hatred of the people who inhabit that land. The conflict thus established parallels that in Ethan, who remains so intensely loyal to the defeated South that he will not accept the authority of Samuel Clayton, captain of the Texas Rangers. Ethan is the ultimate loner, not, as with Cooper's Natty Bumppo, because of a love for the land but because of a strong sense of loss—loss of Mary to his brother, loss of the South, and loss of the beauty once found in the West.

Ethan searches for those things he has lost, a search that appropriately finds its object in a young girl. A defender of virginity, Ethan cannot deal with either the actual fact or the metaphorical implications of Debbie's having become the squaw of Chief Scarface; his response to loss of virginity is to destroy both the individual violated and the source of violation. The title and the plot of the movie finally force us to ask what is the object of Ethan's search—youth? family? daughter?—and why that search is undertaken. Ethan is part of the past, an intense and bitter man who becomes like the savages he hunts.

Set against Ethan's bitterness is the rollicking relationship of Martin Pawley and Laurie Jorgensen. Vera Miles plays Laurie and, in the 1962 *Liberty Valance*, Hallie Stoddard, imaging the appearance in Ford's later work of a woman no longer completely dependent upon male protection. Both Laurie and Hallie pursue and win men considerably different from the now obviously aging John Wayne figure so central throughout Ford's westerns. Martin Pawley and Ransom Stoddard are easterners and young men capable in their own right. For example, in the opening of *The Searchers*, Martin spots a problem with the Indian trail before Ethan does, for the latter is at that moment busily caught up in denouncing Martin for calling him "Uncle." Martin and Ransom are young men characterized as less traditionally masculine than the rugged John Wayne, so the Edenic, beautiful world of the embittered

Ethan Edwards is being replaced by that of a new breed of male (talented but somewhat comic) and female.

When Nora Ericson, in *The Man Who Shot Liberty Valance*, tells her husband to go put his pants on, we find ouselves at the end of the John Ford western. In fact, *Liberty Valance* is a movie about the death of the western, as Ford imagined that story. The movie is therefore appropriately shot in black and white, a fact that in 1962 and after the spectacular color of *Yellow Ribbon* and *The Searchers* certainly calls attention to itself. The color has quite literally gone out of the Ford story. Reinforcing that death, the natural magnificence of Monument Valley is replaced by a setting that forces us to be conscious of its artificiality—even the makeup used for Pompey, Ranse, and Hallie during the opening and closing sequences calls attention to itself. As Robert Ray has discussed, the reverse camera shot of Liberty's death makes it clear that we cannot assume anything about the reliability of what the camera shows.[5] Finally, the major story line is told in flashback, a technique that keeps before us the black-and-white modern world of Senator Ranse Stoddard while pushing the West of Tom Doniphon far into the past. The cruel Liberty Valance is killed, but much continues to trouble the imagination of John Ford. Tom Doniphon (John Wayne), the color and energy of Ford's West, is dead; his coffin occupies center stage.

Ford's movies have significant titles, and *The Man Who Shot Liberty Valance* is no exception. On the surface, the title is ironic, seeming to refer to Ranse Stoddard, though we eventually learn that it was Tom Doniphon who shot Liberty Valance. Both title and movie, while appearing to focus on Ranse and his rise to political power, in reality focus on the demise of Tom and his once colorful world. Equally prominent in the title and the movie is the man Tom shoots, the curiously named Liberty Valance. In spite of the confrontation between them, Doniphon and Valance are part of the same world that has yielded its energy to the law books of Ransom Stoddard. Tom and Liberty, for example, both use their guns to humble Stoddard by spilling a bucket of liquid on him; both expect Ranse to use a gun in self-defense or to get out of town. Ranse, in the restaurant scene, even yells that Tom is no different from Liberty. Thus, when Tom kills Liberty, he kills a central part of his own world, hastening the death that the movie makes the subject of its interest.

And surely we are invited to play with the various implications of the fact that the vicious Valance should be named Liberty.[6] We cheer his death and that of the repression he embodied, but the movie is also concerned about the "liberty" that replaces him. When Pompey, Tom's black companion, forgets the words "that all men are created equal" in his effort to describe Jefferson's document, Ranse notes that "a lot of people forget that line." Further, Maxwell Scott, editor of the *Shinbone Star*, tells Senator Stoddard that he cannot accept the senator's privacy—"purely personal is not good enough for my readers"— and that in fact he has a right to know the story of Tom Doniphon. Finally, when Custis Buck Langhorn is nominated to go to Washington, his supporters celebrate using a horse and cowboy rider to the music of "Home on the Range," but the scene is shot in a narrow hall which emphasizes restriction and confinement. Moments such as these raise questions about the nature of "liberty" in Ranse's world.

In the movie's final moments, Hallie Stoddard speaks of the fact that the wilderness is now a garden and asks her husband "Aren't you proud?" The tone of her voice is absolutely neutral, and we are not surprised. We are not surprised because the line can be uttered in different ways, can underscore achievement or express sorrow. And that ambiguity is a fitting statement for the final effect of *The Man Who Shot Liberty Valance*.

Collectively, these movies, which span the years from 1939 to 1962, describe the imagination of John Ford in its preoccupation with enclosure. Though his imagination is attracted to the color, freedom, and energy of the West, it is committed to enclosing and reshaping wilderness in order to make it safe for young women, families, and Shakespeare. Like Crèvecoeur, Parkman, Brown, Hawthorne, Adams, James, and Faulkner, John Ford finds wilderness stimulating to individual possibility but threatening to civilized values. With *The Searchers* and *The Man Who Shot Liberty Valance*, possibility and threat are integrated in the figure of Ethan Edwards and in the relationship between Doniphon and Valance. Though we feel a loss as color goes out of the West, the movies indicate that without white man's laws and order, the line between individual and savage is indeed very fine.

A sense of loss for a myth of great beauty is the dominant impression created by the western movies of John Ford. With the energy gone, we are left with necessary but troubling questions about the future. Ford's story is thus part of the dominant eastern tradition of Owen Wister and Zane Grey. In contrast, the movies of Sam Peckinpah produce a very different final impression. Peckinpah carries forward that story begun by Lewis Garrard and Mary Austin and developed by Ernest Hemingway and Wright Morris.

1962 was the year of release for both Ford's *Liberty Valance* and Peckinpah's *Ride the High Country*, movies that seem to invite comparison as statements of loss. I have already discussed Ford's movie as one that focuses on the coffin of a man whose image had for two decades been made to represent the West. John Kitses says that "the elegiac tone [in *Ride the High Country*] of an autumnal world marks the passing of the old order."[7] And Paul Seydor finds in the movie's final shot "the effect of loss made visually poignant by the absence of Gil in the frame as Steve is left alone to look for one last time at the western horizon before turning slowly and lowering himself to the ground and to death."[8] Such comments urge a similarity between Ford and Peckinpah's concern with loss, but I do not find them accurate statements of what happens in this early expression of Peckinpah's imagination.[9]

In the introduction to the second chapter of this study, I indicate that what characterizes the noncanonical imagination is a rejection of eastern enclosures, both physical and mental, and a struggle to narrate the fascination with space and to thereby accept and draw upon the possibilities of wilderness. The effort to narrate exploration of, rather than taming of, the frontier marks the work of this imagination. Western "frontier" is an area of continual opening rather than a receding point between civilization and wilderness. I began with landscape because it is the land that initially draws the eye out into its act of exploration. In Mary Austin and Ernest Hemingway, land and the rhythms of the land are primary; in Guthrie and Fergusson, an individual struggles to relate his life to the physical environment; and Clark's *The Ox-Bow Incident* explores human relationships in the new high country. Exploration of a continually opening frontier is not synonymous with mapping out and taming the land. In these terms Sam Peckinpah's imagination is a crucial part of spatial exploration. Beginning with the land, Peckinpah emphasizes a visual world, using primarily images rather than ideas. He moves from one moment of possibility to another, less interested in past or future than in the multiple directions of an ever-changing present. And given Peckinpah's western heritage, it would indeed be surprising if he and the eastern John Ford told the same story.

What discussions of *Ride the High Country* fail to see in the movie is the centrality of Heck Longtree. If we focus on the story of the old-timers Gil Westrum and Steve Judd, making the romance of Heck and Elsa Knudson a conventional subplot, then the dying of Steve in the final frame does indeed conclude a story of loss.[10] However, when we look at the movie, we see that it involves the four characters, particularly the three men, equally. The story that emerges, then, transfers power from one generation to another. Peckinpah has been quoted in several places saying that "I have never made a 'Western.' I have made a lot of films about men on horseback."[11] The distinction is important, for it indicates that Peckinpah's movies are more about people within a physical world than about celebrating any particular region. The distinction is also useful in interpreting *Ride the High Country*, which is not a conventional western but a movie about men on horseback. It is not a story of the lost wonder that was the West; it is, rather, one of young people taking the reins of power from an aging generation, discovering the land, and beginning to explore their "place" within it.

Both *She Wore a Yellow Ribbon* and *The Searchers* set the image of the aging John Wayne against that of a young man who would be the future. Taking Martin Pawley (*Searchers*) as an example and comparing him with Heck Longtree, we find a considerable difference between Ford's and Peckinpah's visions of the future. Martin Pawley is likable and talented, but he is not John Wayne—few men are. Martin is a somewhat comic figure, easily manipulated by women—the Indian Look and Laurie Jorgensen. No one need feel depressed about a future of people like Martin and Laurie, but the movie makes clear that the world of Ethan Edwards is over. Heck Longtree is also likable and talented, but he is going to be able to build upon the values of Steve Judd. More than anyone else in *High Country*, Heck grows during the course of the movie. In many ways, the movie is his story and is therefore a story of growth that compensates for the necessary loss through death that occurs at the end. When Heck is first introduced to Steve Judd, the camera does everything it can to show that Heck has no

interest in looking at Steve; Heck's eyes follow a shapely young wait-
ress. Verbally he returns the matter-of-fact introduction, but visually
his eyes demonstrate an interest in sex. During the course of the movie,
Heck's eyes focus more and more on Steve, finally seeing the values
embodied in that aging man. Judd's encounter with the Samsons,
the father and son who run the bank and hire Judd, emphasizes that
Steve's eyes are getting old and that eyesight is crucial to survival.
Consequently, to have Heck's eyes finally see both the excitement of a
woman's body and the strengths of Steve Judd indicates that his rising
up from the death of Judd in no way constitutes loss.

Steve Judd frequently refers to Heck as "Son": "No use tormenting
yourself, Son," he says when Elsa is being married to Billy Hammond.
And Heck is a son capable of learning; returning his gun to Judd,
Heck says, "Sorry, Mr. Judd. I guess I was showing off." With that
father-son relationship in contrast to the stultifying relationships of
the Samsons or of Joshua Knudson and Elsa, the dying of Judd finally
opens the future for Heck. [12] And Heck has always shown himself anxious to take advantage of openings: the camel race, Gil Westrum's pro-
posal of robbery, Elsa's apparent willingness to intimacy. The first visit
to Elsa's house contains a scene shot with Elsa inside (her father's
world is one of the enclosing structures) washing dishes beside an
open window. Suddenly Heck's head and shoulders appear through
the window, and he invites Elsa to meet him outside. His willingness
to take advantage of openings together with his growing willingness
to see the strengths of Steve Judd establish Heck as the figure through
whom this movie moves toward a beginning.

The camera has been active from the opening frame. The camera
does not just give us an angle from which we can watch the action;
it actively searches out, explores the world around it. This quality is
particularly evident in the opening exploration of the high country's
green land, in the early street scenes, in the crowd shots at Kate's Place
in Coarsegold, and in the discovery of Knudson's dead body. And
when death pulls Steve Judd to the ground in the final frame, the
camera does not freeze on a dead body; it moves up, back to the green
of the high country. The lowering body thus implies that we are on the
verge of seeing something rise. That something need not necessarily
be Heck, but the sexual juices stirring in the characters, the activity of
the camera, and the impressive growth of both Heck and Elsa suggest

that *Ride the High Country* is a story of the integral bond between death and new life.

Major Dundee (1964) is a story of union, in every sense of the word.[13] In fact, what carries through between *High Country* and *Major Dundee* is Peckinpah's vision of union. The movie opens with a series of divisions that dominate much of the story's surface: verbal/visual; soldier/Indian; Union/Confederate; Dundee/Tyreen. The list could be extended—white/black; Scottish/Irish; male/female; European/American; United States/Mexico—but the striking characteristic of the movie is that it is not a story of confrontation and division. In spite of seemingly endless individual confrontations, overriding everything is the impulse to union. Consequently, setting the story in 1864–65, when the Civil War was drawing to its close, emphasizes both the problem attacked and the effort being made during the movie. The story ends April 19, 1865, four days after the death of Lincoln, a time in America of needed healing.

The initial shot in *Major Dundee* has Corporal Ryan's *Journal* being opened and words spread out before us. We do not move from words to image; rather, the visual burns through the page, flames consuming words and leaving us with events. The effort to burn away divisive intellectual constructs is the imaginative thrust propelling the movie. Thus, after the opening scenes of destruction, the Apache Sierra Charriba asks defiantly, "Who will you send against me now?" and the movie itself answers with the words of the title and the background song, "Fall in Behind the Major." Words, music, and images—an integrated effort—respond to Charriba's defiance and destruction. As the song concludes, falling in behind the major is essential for the individuals to get home again.

Probably the line repeated most frequently throughout the movie is given initially as the Confederate Ben Tyreen's condition for working with the Yankee Amos Dundee: "Until the Apache is taken or destroyed." Literally, of course, the line has only one meaning, but as the movie progresses and the line is repeated, who or what "Apache" signifies begins to seem less certain. This is, after all, a border story, a story about thieves, deserters, renegades, blacks, and gentlemen of the South who leave the territory of the United States and cross the border into Mexico, chasing the Apache. The initial reason for the chase, to rescue captured children, is quickly disposed of as the children return and are sent north. Thus we have to ask about the concerns that really motivate the movie, Major Dundee, and his troops as they cross the border to take or destroy the Apache.

Movement into Mexico strips away external authority, so the chaotic band and the individuals within it are on their own. Unity can no longer be imposed; conditions now lay bare the dangerously divisive nature of their enterprise. North of the border, Dundee's authority is supported by rank and the superior Union force within his fort. South of the border, authority and rank crumble. When Lieutenant Graham tries to get the men together to march, chaos and confusion surround his assertion of authority by rank, and he is ineffectual, if humorous. No external authority is in place to keep Captain Tyreen and his Confederates from fleeing to join other Confederate troops, but they do not desert because Tyreen has given Dundee his word. Once the men are over the border, the destructive implications of their division become immediately evident when racial conflict erupts. "Until the Apache is taken or destroyed" begins to sound as though it were directed at a savagery at the core of the men, individually and collectively, that must be confronted before union can become a possibility.

Confronting savagery is central to the movies of John Ford as well as Sam Peckinpah, but the differences between the two are important. In Ford, savage wilderness is a direct threat to civilized values, and the threat must be met by the forces of law and order. The Cathy Downs/Shirley Temple/Natalie Wood figures must be protected from something external to them. In Peckinpah, savagery is not an evil to be held outside the walls of civilization but a distortion of internal energy. That energy therefore needs to be transformed from its destructive to its constructive possibilities. Women play a role in Peckinpah's movies unlike that in Ford's. The image of a woman like Senta Berger (Teresa Santiago in *Major Dundee*) contrasts sharply with the image of Cathy Downs or Shirley Temple. Berger's body is lush, and despite her declaration that the soldiers will not find what they want in the village, her gesture of opening her shawl indicates that they will find at least what she has to give. Berger's standing beside the village's ruined columns nicely images the vitality, the life existing within her that will replace impermanent efforts to build structures or violent efforts to destroy. In Ford's *Fort Apache*, Tombstone, Arizona, offers law and order and a church to counter the surrounding barren wasteland; in *Major Dundee*, the Mexican village offers flesh-and-blood people—their joys and their love. A different kind of energy exists in the latter—a natural energy referred to by Teresa when she says that she is with Major Dundee because she has seen too much dying, that she wants them both to "feel alive."

Major Dundee concludes with the remnant of the army uniting under Dundee's command and under the colors of the Union to battle European forces in Mexico before moving back into Texas. The movie ends as they slowly ride away from us, their faces weary—in particular that of Sergeant Chillum (Ben Johnson). Only one song is played, whereas earlier, Union and Confederate singing had fought for center stage. Four years later, Peckinpah's next movie, *The Wild Bunch* (1969), opens with a group of men riding toward the camera. Ben Johnson's face (now Tector Gorch) effects the carryover between the two bunches of men. After *The Wild Bunch*, *The Ballad of Cable Hogue* (1970) will move us from the group to the single individual; but before the individual is allowed to emerge, our attention is focused on the wildness of the group.

Like *Major Dundee*, *The Wild Bunch* opens with a shot that indicates the movie is going to be concerned with the tension between and the transformation of an old form to a new one. In *Major Dundee*, the words of Ryan's *Journal* were burned through by images that carried the movie until the final shot, when the *Journal* is closed. The opening of *The Wild Bunch* unites the active camera of *Ride the High Country* and the transformed medium of *Major Dundee*. Now the opening shots establish a defined and frozen world in conflict with movement. We first see a black-and-white still image of the bunch. The still then breaks into color and movement. The camera then immediately moves off center, the image freezes once again into black and white, and the words *The Wild Bunch* appear. As though searching for the activity of the individuals in the bunch, the camera moves back to center on the frozen image, and once again color and activity appear. This interchange continues between the verbal black-and-white freezing and the effort of the camera to find faces. The extent of the freezing is most apparent when the bunch finally enters the town of Starbuck and the voice of the revival preacher rings out in the background; even the preacher's voice is stilled when the freezing occurs ("Now, folks . . ."), and it picks up exactly where it left off when action returns (". . . that's from the good book"). The centering action of the camera is evident when children playing with a scorpion and ants become the focus of its interest—even their faces are searched by the moving camera. The opening of *The Wild Bunch* therefore values activity, color, and the individual, and that valuing is going to be the concern of the entire movie. Not until the next movie will our attention be entirely on an individual, although during *The Wild Bunch* we do search for individuals within the bunch. That kind of exploration constitutes the primary western element in the imagination of Sam Peckinpah.

We also search for the source of the bunch's wildness, a search made more interesting with John Ford and Mary Austin in mind. The imagination of Ford would never value the bunch; towns and forts are central to the stability of Ford's world. In Peckinpah, however, towns are sterile, and the forces of law and order are cruel and despotic. Austin said in *The Land of Little Rain* that "lawlessness" was a favorite topic of the eastern imagination in depicting the West, but the West had laws of its own. In the movies of Peckinpah, the lawlessness of civilized stability presents a center of attention. In *The Wild Bunch*, Harrigan of the railroad and Mapache of the Federales are the representatives of law and order, but they are vicious and corrupt. In this context, the wildness of the bunch seems more an expression of frustrated internal energies than a destructive principle harmful to civilization. The wildness of the bunch connects most closely with the lush bodies of the Mexican women, suggesting that in these two forces—energy and flesh—lie the dynamics of life. The bunch thus seems wild only to someone like Harrigan, for example, who must destroy it if his railroad empire can exist without threat. Neither in their home base nor in Angel's village is the bunch truly wild.

Many readers may feel that I am downplaying the violence in Peckinpah's work. This response, with which I do not agree, is not surprising: readers of canonical American literature, who have been trained in certain expectations and assumptions, are going to be made uncomfortable by many products of the western imagination. To them, *The Land of Little Rain* lacks form; *Green Hills of Africa* is self-indulgent posturing; *The Home Place* spreads itself too thin between text and photos; *This House of Sky* offers little more than pleasant biography; and the movies of Sam Peckinpah are politically irresponsible in their celebration of violence. I noted earlier that readers of *Main-Travelled Roads* have consistently failed to respond to the work's optimistic elements, and viewers who come away from Peckinpah's movies concerned about the violence they portray have similarly overlooked the laughter and the joy that equally characterize his work.

The common denominator running through many eastern responses to western narrative is the sense that something in the work does not come up to the expectations or standards of canonical narrative. However, given that the enclosed stance of canonical work develops from the conviction that the demands of the physical world run counter to the best possibilities of contemporary civilization, I would argue that western literature's "failure" is that it is not as negative as is traditional literature about the physical world. To the contrary, the westerner seems to be moving in the direction of sharing with the Indian and the Chicano an appreciation of the relationships among members of an environment. Instead of building "a world elsewhere" designed to preserve egos and a fixed set of values, as is amply demonstrated in Francis Parkman's *The Oregon Trail*, the western imagination asks about individual "place" within ecosystems. Because the ecosystems themselves contain violence, violence in Cooper or Austin or Fergusson or Hemingway or Morris or Peckinpah should be neither surprising nor troubling.

Building "a world elsewhere" is not a violent act; if anything, it seeks to avoid those activities of the physical world that appear unseemly to civilized tastes. There is not much that one might speak of as violent in Hawthorne or James; there is, of course, much personal and social cruelty, but not much physical violence. One must argue for the opposite in western work—violence occurs, but without any corresponding cruelty. Life is by nature a violent process; life can only take place if individual units of energy are consumed and transformed. In *Walden* the narrator speaks of chastity as the "flowering" of man—a conception that eliminates sexual intercourse or other forms of gross feeding and slights the physical and violent aspects of human life. In contrast, violence appears in western art as the necessary outcome of either of two processes: the natural activity of the physical world (as in *The Land of Little Rain*, *Green Hills of Africa*, and *Mountain Man*) or the suppression of natural impulses by an enclosing set of structures (as in *The Last of the Mohicans*, *In Our Time*, and *In Orbit*).

The movies of Sam Peckinpah portray both violent processes. In John Ford's work, violence occurs when white society goes out to tame the physical world, *tame* being a code word for *destroy*. When the cavalry arrives to save the day in *Stagecoach*, for example, it does so by obliterating the Indians—they completely vanish from the screen. In Ford's movies, the desire to wipe out resistance to the onrushing, enclosing civilization justifies violence. It seems to me rather curious that our society understands and applauds such acts. In a world comprehended in terms of right/wrong, good/evil, we support the effort of good to destroy evil using any means at hand—and evil is usually understood to be anything that is not what we define as good. This kind of violence, though unfortunate, we argue, is essential to protect the fragile flower of civilization. From this perspective, which accepts and perhaps appreciates violence in Ford, violent acts in Peckinpah seem at best extraneous, at worst celebrated.

In Peckinpah's movies, violence explodes out of situations that require violent reaction. The explosion is usually the result of cruelty that seems bent on destroying the natural world. In this, violence in Peckinpah's films is similar to the violence at the center of *The Last of the Mohicans*: one can rape and pillage only so long before the victims begin to take action. The cruelty imposed on the young couple in Peckinpah's *Straw Dogs* is another case in point: sooner or later, the gentle mathematics professor will explode in anger. The opening of *The Wild Bunch* concentrates on a group of children delighting in their torture of insects. Moments later, Harrigan's forces open fire on the bunch, and the act leads to the violence that explodes in the town of Starbuck.

The bunch is out of date in the modern world (the movie is a border story), and, like the tortured scorpion, they will be crushed by the larger forces of society, in their case the railroad and the Federales. Peckinpah's stories frequently portray an older order being sloughed off, stories in which neither the representatives of the old nor the representatives of the new can really be termed "good guys." It is simply the sloughing that merits the attention of the movie, and the sloughing has violence built into its core. We watch worlds transit from old to new in everything from *One-Eyed Jacks* to *Convoy*, and the changes always involve resistance, force, and violence.

The violence that change involves is especially well portrayed in

Peckinpah's *The Wild Bunch*, in which wildness provides a countering force to the repression imposed by so many groups in the movie, from a group promoting temperance to a group promoting Nazism. Whatever energies potentially unite them, the wild bunch is appropriately named, for they, like Amos Dundee's army, continually threaten to come apart. And like Dundee, their leader, Pike Bishop, struggles to keep them together. Ultimately, that internal wildness is more of a threat to their existence than the external pressure exerted by Harrigan or Mapache. In spite of the chaos that comes early in the movie when they discover that they have been tricked, the bunch gradually unites around the values of Pike Bishop. Like Steve Judd in *Ride the High Country*, Pike is aging in body but not in spirit; even the Gorch brothers can see in him the qualities that hold them all together, as is particularly evident in the scene that concludes the chaos of tumbling horses and men after lines became tangled. After Pike tells them that if they can't stick together, they're finished, the bunch watches him painfully mount his horse and ride away. They follow that image.[14] And also like Steve Judd, Pike Bishop dies, and his comrades die. The bunch is obliterated at the end of the movie in a scene of uncontrolled violence. Not loss, however, but transformation from old to new is Peckinpah's story. In *The Wild Bunch* that transformation is evidenced in the several scenes of laughter, a bursting forth of an internal joy that goes beyond the immediate individual, becomes contagious, and pulls in others. When Mapache or the body robbers who follow Deke Thornton laugh, the laughter is cruel and self-centered. Instead of uniting others, it separates them. But not so the laughter of the bunch: Freddie Sikes, the old-timer in the Bunch, begins the laughter after Harrigan's trick of substituting washers for gold has threatened Pike's authority, and it is laughter directed at themselves rather than at someone else. Laughter and childish playing recur frequently. And laughter is the image we are left with at the end after Freddie suggests to Deke that they reunite because they "got some work to do."

The laughter and that final reunion indicate that the transformation, visualized in the opening effort of the camera to seek out faces and turn still photographs into moving images, has worked and is continuing to work. For all the violence, perhaps because of the violence, laughter explodes out of this movie; in spite of the deaths of Pike and his men, a new bunch has work to do.

Peckinpah's imagination also has work to do, more territory to explore, carrying us forward to *The Ballad of Cable Hogue* (1970). The title of *Cable Hogue* indicates that earlier efforts of the camera to find the individual have been completed and that the laughter that rose out of previous violence will be an underlying force in *Cable Hogue*.[15] This movie is the narrative song of a particular individual thrust out of an initial three-man "bunch" who stumbles onto a source of nourishment after yielding up his ego; his final rejection of the desire for revenge makes possible the movement outward from Cable Springs that concludes the movie.

Cable's name indicates that he is a figure who unites. Cable pulls himself together; he establishes an important tie with Hildy; and he connects the efforts in earlier movies to find the individual and in the later movies to ask what that individual might be capable of. This is a movie, therefore, that culminates previous actions in Peckinpah and establishes the possibility of throwing those actions forward.

As one might expect in Peckinpah, the opening shots point the direction of the movie. Instead of burning away or transforming one medium into another, *Cable Hogue* opens with the individual directly confronting the natural world: Cable—and the camera—eyeing a Gila monster. Mary Austin's distinction between westerners' and easterners' view of the land is again useful because Cable is an individual who uses his eyes. He sees the lizard as a needed source of food, in contrast to his partners, who blast it into useless pieces; Cable then discovers that the desert is not ten million gallons of sand, as Bowen and Taggart say; and after discovering water, he looks in both directions along the stage route and "sees" the future transit along that highway and the future need for his water. He also sees Hildy, first with his eyes locked on her breasts and later as the person that she is—"Lady, nobody ever seen you before."

There is a great deal, of course, that Cable does not see or understand. He accidentally stumbles onto the desert water, does not think about filing a claim, cannot read, and has never before seen a car. He is therefore not unlike Pike Bishop, who stumbles into a woman carrying packages as the bunch prepares to rob Starbuck, but both Pike and Cable are able to adjust to opportunity within a given set of circumstances. As a consequence, the narratives of both the bunch and Cable Hogue do not have the linear plot usually employed by Ford and rejected by such midwesterners as Anderson, Hemingway, and Morris. In *Stagecoach*, for example, we know that the effort will be to get a certain number of people by stagecoach to Lordsburg; in *The Searchers*, it will be to find Debbie Edwards; and in *The Man Who Shot Liberty Valance*, it will be to find out what really happened to Tom Doniphon. However, something quite different is working in *The Wild Bunch* and *The Ballad of Cable Hogue*. Though both movies establish early an external plot—Deke Thornton hunting the bunch, Cable seeking revenge—in neither case is that external plot particularly relevant to later events. Instead, events spring internally from previous events. Both Pike and Cable are particularly talented at looking into the moment and seizing upon possibility. The bunch, for example, is not running from Deke; instead, they pick up on Angel's problem with Teresa and his village's problem with the Federales and begin a new adventure. Then, when the opportunity presents itself, they take to the idea of robbing the train. In this, Pike contrasts with Angel, who is so controlled by his desire for revenge that he allows externals to destroy him.

Similarly, Cable Hogue seizes upon a series of accidents to build a flourishing business. Events—such as both appearances of Hildy at Cable Springs—seem to happen fortuitously. We watch Cable's reaction to events; we do not give thought to an overarching plan and are therefore momentarily puzzled by Cable's statement about midway through the movie that he cannot leave with Hildy until "they" return. "They" are Taggart and Bowen, the partners who earlier deserted Cable, but most viewers would feel that Cable has long forgotten them—he has not mentioned them, nor has he been hunting them. In fact, the absence of plot and the presence of the fortuitous are in large part responsible for the lack of public interest in the movie, but to fault the movie for these two characteristics is to miss the importance in Peckinpah of the ability to see possibility inherent in each moment, each individual. Cable's initial concentration on Hildy's breasts, for example, is neither extraneous nor casual plotting; his developing ability to see her as a person is the essence of Cable's story.

As a consequence of being committed to the possibilities of the moment, Cable is not locked into Cable Springs. He gives up not only his desire for revenge against Taggart and Bowen but also Cable Springs. When Hildy returns, Cable is ready to move on, to move with her into new opportunity. That he does not understand the mechanics of the automobile leads to his death and indicates his limitations in the modern world, but his death is not important, and we do not even see him die; he is just gone. Early in the movie, the banker, Cushing, asks about Cable's collateral, and Cable responds, "I'm worth something, ain't I?" At the end, the Reverend Joshua Sloan talks about Cable's worth, and one can argue that Cable's developing worth as a source of value to others has been the focus of the entire movie. The final words are given to his worth; the final images are of machines and people moving out of Cable Springs in several directions as a coyote draws near to drink of the water. The song of Cable Hogue is thus the song of an individual who could find water where others could not, whose joy in life's possibilities is passed on to others. Appropriately, therefore, the concluding song ends with the line, "I'll see what tomorrow will bring."

As my concern has been to contrast two different imaginations rather than detail the complete work of Ford or Peckinpah, I need only briefly mention Peckinpah's films that follow *The Ballad of Cable Hogue*. *Straw Dogs* (1971), *Junior Bonner* (1972), and *The Getaway* (1972) pick up the image of the car, which concludes *Cable Hogue*. And the figure of Kris Kristofferson in both *Pat Garrett and Billy the Kid* (1973) and *Convoy* (1978) integrates the image of the dying horse outlaw and that of the emerging vehicle outlaw. The movies, in other words, continue Peckinpah's interest in exploring the continually opening frontier, in seeing "what tomorrow will bring."

Through the movies of Ford and Peckinpah, I have tried to indicate that in these two men who focus on the common image of the West we have radically different imaginations at work. The resulting stories reflect those characteristics of enclosure and space that I have detailed throughout this book. What is important is not the valuing of one perception over another but the recognizing what necessarily happens when we assume that in America only one imagination has a story to tell. To prefer the movies of John Ford, as traditionalists do, or to regard the work of Sam Peckinpah as politically irresponsible is to see one imagination only through another's eyes and to miss a dynamic, "lawless" story that has been developing in America for almost two centuries. Eastern perceptions such as those of Parkman, James, Faulkner, and Ford are greatly troubled by wilderness and turn to the politically and culturally "responsible" values that created civilization as the East knows it, but other imaginations are also at work, fascinated with both the risks and the possibilities of "what tomorrow will bring."

Notes

INTRODUCTION

1. Given the overall movement I describe in Melville—from unknown to known worlds and from exploration to constriction—I find an interesting parallel in Nina Baym's discussion of Melville's shifting attitude toward fiction: "I reason that, given Melville's Emerson-derived notion of language as proceeding from a divine Author or namer, the loss of belief in an Absolute entailed the loss not only of truth in the universe but also coherence and meaning in language. In *Moby-Dick* we are poised on the brink of an awareness of these losses; in *Pierre* we have tumbled into the abyss. . . . His somewhat more favorable judgment of *White-Jacket* [vs. *Redburn*] may be similarly attributed to its greater departure from narrative line and the controls of the fictional situation" ("Melville's Quarrel with Fiction," pp. 910, 914).

2. An assertion of common ground between North and South is certainly going to generate disagreement. C. Hugh Holman, for example, speaks of the southerner as "archetypal man sharply at variance with the standard American view" in that "he has offered himself as a scapegoat for the frustrations and guilts of modern America" ("The Southerner as Writer," p. 191). C. Vann Woodward, in "The Southern Ethic in a Puritan World," is another who seeks to define southern distinctiveness.

However, some critics would agree that the parallels between North and South are many. Perry Miller, in *Errand into the Wilderness*, develops the fact of common English roots in North and South. David M. Potter, in "The Enigma of the South," argues that the traditional equation between southernism and agrarianism is false, that a commercial spirit in fact underlies both northern and southern economies. More recently, Fred Hobson begins his *Tell about the South* by questioning the idea of southern distinctiveness: "Whatever their differences, however, all these writers [those he is about to discuss] showed a belief in the uniqueness of southern history, a conviction that the South is substantially different from the rest of the United States. . . . And they believed not only in the uniqueness but in the importance of that uniqueness—which is to say that these particular Southerners seem rarely or never to have entertained the secret doubt that Southern scholars, no matter how committed to the task, sometimes have: that the South's uniqueness may not really be as important as its similarities to the rest of the Union" (p. 7).

Lewis P. Simpson, in *The Dispossessed Garden*, had earlier found one such similarity in dispossession, the common experience of the northerner and southerner.

From all the material on the subject, one might conclude, at the very least, that both northerner and southerner wrap their economic impulses in a mantle of national piety. See also Karanikas, *Tillers of a Myth*.

3. Part of the problem I hope to address was suggested to me by Russel Nye. As a midwesterner, he indicated that eastern critics have consistently misread Hamlin Garland's *Main-Travelled Roads*. Midwesterners, he said, do not see the scholarly emphasis on pessimism as justified.

CHAPTER 1

1. James, *The Notebooks of Henry James*, p. 316.

2. Richard Poirier has extended James's fascination with enclosure to a more general discussion in *A World Elsewhere: The Place of Style in American Literature*. He argues that through stylistic enclosure the American writer explores New World possibility: "The great works of American literature are alive with the effort to stabilize certain feelings and attitudes that have, as it were, no place in the world" (*A World Elsewhere*, p. ix). "Metaphors of 'building,' " "structures," and "enclosure" dominate American writing, according to Poirier. I certainly agree with his emphasis on enclosure, but what particularly fascinates and troubles me about his argument is its claim to be inclusive of the "most exciting American books," when, in fact, he means *eastern* American writing—so eastern that he even discusses the work of Jane Austen. That inclusion is not surprising given that Poirier regards American literature as "a distinctive American tradition within English literature" (ibid., p. 5).

Poirier would probably be quick to point out that his book is a study of the relationship between freedom and imaginative enclosure, but I want to emphasize that Poirier examines a particular kind of relationship, an eastern relationship. *A World Elsewhere* is an important book within the context of the East, but its thesis is highly problematic when imposed on all American writing. "Expansive characters," says Poirier, "in Cooper or Emerson, Melville, James, or Fitzgerald are thus convinced as if by history of the practical possibility of enclosing the world in their imaginations," an act which Poirier sees as an extension of English romantic poetry into American prose (ibid., p. 3).

My point about the unfortunate tendency of many scholars to equate "eastern" with "American" may also be noted in the title and introduction to Charles Berryman's *From Wilderness to Wasteland: The Trial of the Puritan God in the American Imagination*. Berryman says that his "central interest is the American imagination itself" (p. ix), but the individuals discussed make the book entirely eastern in content. From my perspective, this traditional story might more appropriately be described as moving from distrusted wilderness to experienced wasteland.

3. Numerous works discuss the image of the New World Eden. See, for example, Jones, *O Strange New World*; Sanford, *Quest for Paradise*; Lewis, *The American Adam*; Marx, *The Machine in the Garden*; Fryer, *Faces of Eve*; and Spengemann, *The Adventurous Muse*. In addition, Stewart's *The Enclosed Garden* discusses the images of gardens and enclosure in seventeenth-century English poetry. To many, America symbolized the potential extension of those gardens.

4. Variations of the importance of a wilderness idea are discussed in Nash, *Wilderness and the American Mind*; Kolodny, *The Lay of the Land*; and Slotkin, *Regeneration through Violence*.

5. Spengemann, *The Adventurous Muse*, pp. 23–24.

6. Davis, *Intellectual Life in the Colonial South*, 1:6–7.

7. This point is developed by Simpson in *The Dispossessed Garden*.

8. Stewart's *The Enclosed Garden* examines the security provided by verbal enclosures in seventeenth-century English poetry. Chapter 1 of Ziff's *Puritanism in America* provides the intellectual background of the Puritan mind, which, as William Ames presented it, came to value verbal enclosures. Thus in several senses, a man's word became his bond. In Genesis, God gives form to the void through language. As the means of creation, the Word is the divine source of power. Thus the Word of God should serve as a stimulus to the creative use of human words, God's narrative as a stimulus to human narrative. According to William Carlos Williams, "The jargon of God . . . was their dialect by which they kept themselves surrounded as with a palisade" (*In the American Grain*, p. 64).

9. For discussions of verbal structures in American Puritan poetry see Keller, *The Example of Edward Taylor*; Daly, *God's Altar*; and Scheick, *The Will and the Word*.

10. Slotkin, *The Fatal Environment*, p. 63.

11. The text I am using appears in Rowlandson, *The Sovereignty and Goodness of God*, in *Held Captive by Indians: Selected Narratives, 1642–1836*, ed. VanDerBeets.

12. Slotkin, *Regeneration through Violence*, p. 110.

13. McIlwaine, *The Southern Poor-White from Lubberland to Tobacco Road*, p. 17.

14. William Alexander Caruthers's *The Knights of the Golden Horse-Shoe* (1845) provides a good example. The story opens with the description of a house that "commanded a fine prospect of the Chesapeake Bay" and was surrounded by a "beautiful green lawn" ending in a "bubbling brook." The story then moves inside, where close attention is paid to the building's physical structure and the conversation of those who live there. Dialogue dominates the narrative, and even when the action moves outdoors, only the most generalized description is offered: "The encampment was pitched upon a beautiful plain, in that region of country now called Albemarle, one of the most charming spots in America. The mountains were distinctly in view, on more sides than one, but the dark blue boundaries of the horizon in the West, were apparently as far off as ever" (p. 209).

15. For a fuller discussion of these points, see my essays "Transformation in *Wieland*" and "The Two Portraits in *Wieland*."

16. Blackmur, *Henry Adams*, pp. 24–25.

17. Stone, *Autobiographical Occasions and Original Acts*, p. 46.

18. Faulkner, *Faulkner in the University*, p. 2.

19. Ibid., p. 279.

CHAPTER 2

1. Parkman, *The Oregon Trail*, chap. 2. For a complete discussion of the several editions of *The Oregon Trail*, see the text edited and introduced by E. N. Feltskog. I prefer to work with the 1849 edition chosen by David Levin.

2. Whitehead's discussion of this term occurs in both *Science and the Modern World* and *Process and Reality*.

3. At the 1987 convention of the Western Literature Association in Lincoln, Nebraska, in a talk entitled "Responsibilities of a Western Critic," Simonson argued that "place" should be understood not simply in horizontal geographical terms but with the vertical implications of how man relates to other members of fragile ecological systems. I also refer the reader to remarks by Richard W. Etulain on the continuities between eastern and western American writing; see his "Frontier and Region in Western Literature."

4. Hill's introduction to Twain, *Roughing It*, p. 22.

5. Richter, *The Trees*, pp. 8, 11.

6. In *The Novel of the American West*, John R. Milton discusses symbols common in East and West: "The forest as symbol of the darkness of man, of evil, or of ignorance and mystery, may well be an early indication of one view of the wilderness later on during the frontier movement. However, since much of the West is open land, the symbols did not survive in quite the same way as they did in portions of the South or New England" (p. 81). Regarding enclosure, Milton says: "In the literature of the West, partly because of the lingering frontier influence and partly because of the additional space, there has been less housing (Los Angeles excepted, of course) and more moving. The space is one determinant; there is room to move around in" (p. 90). For a discussion of this topic in Canadian prairie fiction, see Picou, *Vertical Man/Horizontal World*.

7. Ratification dates for states' admission to the Union indicate that settlement occurred later in the plains than in the Far West: 1815–50 was the period of major settlement in Ohio, Illinois, Indiana, and Iowa; 1840–60 in California and Oregon; 1860–90 in Nebraska, Colorado, Wyoming, the Dakotas, and Oklahoma. Not surprisingly, the transcontinental railroad was initially planned as a method of leaping the vast plains.

8. Wayne Franklin describes Magua, the vengeful Iroquois, as a manifestation of the violated wilderness: "Magua gives the challenge of the forest to the Europeans who enter it a human intensity; he is the setting concentrated and given the power to act on them" (*The New World of James Fenimore Cooper*, p. 224). Kolodny also discusses the implications of rape in *The Lay of the Land*.

9. Peck in *A World by Itself* describes *The Last of the Mohicans* as a story without a center, a narrative that "seems to be ordered on the basis of constant motion" (p. 92). Initially, that motion is in search of a father, concluding with the "necessary" destruction of Munro's world and the consequent movement into "a region beyond the landscape of difficulty" (ibid., p. 119). See also Slotkin's *Regeneration through Violence*.

10. E. N. Feltskog's introduction to the text presents the strongest defense of Parkman and surveys most of the material relevant to an understanding of Parkman's ideas about and attitudes toward the West. Drawing on Otis A. Pease's *Parkman's History: The Historian as Literary Artist*, Feltskog concludes: "As Otis A. Pease suggests, much of the emphasis in *The Oregon Trail* falls upon the relationship of the plainsman to weather and landscape. Thus, it seems intellectually more honest to judge Parkman on what he did see and what he did achieve with his wilderness education than to blame him for errors of judgment and perspective which only time would disclose" (pp. 40a–41a).

Both before and after Feltskog, many critics have been more negative. See De Voto, *The Year of Decision, 1846*, and Smith, *Virgin Land: The American West as Symbol and Myth*. More recent is John R. Milton's comment that "Parkman's Boston Brahmin background kept him from putting his experiences into really significant terms: he could not find the language he needed to confront and convey the extent, solitude, and wildness of the West" (*The Novel of the American West*, p. 75).

11. This split between viewing the West as romantic and viewing the East as superior suggests both that Parkman did not know how he wanted to relate to the West and that in many ways a central subject of his text is his ambivalence about the East. Neither position—romantic West or superior East—bespeaks a perceiver willing to be receptive to the West.

12. Certainly the juxtaposition of material creates structural irony, so Parkman may have seen the comic implications of the scene, but it is never more than comic and does not lead to questioning of values. Speaking of excised passages from the

original journal, Feltskog says that they "emphasize even more strongly a number of unresolved paradoxes which the present text of *The Oregon Trail* still clearly shows. The East—and especially New England—is a haven of peace and rest; there Nature is beneficent and healing, and civilization holds men in its firm support. The West is destructive; it brutalizes white men and Indians alike and reduces civilization to a mocking memory" (p. 50a).

13. See Feltskog, in Parkman, *The Oregon Trail* (1969), pp. 43a–44a.
14. Levin, in Parkman, *The Oregon Trail* (1982), p. 21.
15. Garrard, *Wah-to-yah and the Taos Trail*, pp. xiv–xv.
16. Milton, *The Novel of the American West*, p. 74.

CHAPTER 3

1. Ingram, *Representative Short Story Cycles of the Twentieth Century*. John R. Milton discusses form in western writing in *The Novel of the American West*, distinguishing between eastern fiction ("Form is intensive. Novel begins on surface of character and plot and digs in, like peeling layers off an onion. Intensive like the crowded city") and western fiction ("Form is expansive. Novel opens out from character into action, consciousness, moral awareness. Expansive like the open land") (p. 59).
2. Early naturalistic interpretations of Garland's work were presented by Åhnebrink, *The Beginnings of Naturalism in American Fiction*, pp. 63–89, and Walcutt, *American Literary Naturalism*, pp. 53–63.
3. Austin, *The American Rhythm*, p. 9.
4. "In answer to all her critics, Mary replied that she had been misunderstood. She had never said that Indian verse had directly influenced American poetry, but that both had been influenced by common factors in their rhythmic environment" (Pearce, *Mary Hunter Austin*, p. 117).
5. "Central to her vision was the conviction that the land and the people who inhabited it were intricately bound together. . . . She wanted to know how the spirit of man and the creative spirit of the land were welded together to form culture" (Ruppert, "Mary Austin's Landscape Line," p. 377).
6. I find particularly instructive in approaching Sherwood Anderson the comments of David D. Anderson, who argues that critics have long misread Anderson's work:

> In that year [1921] he was enshrined in the Eastern critics' favorite interpretation of the literature that was coming out of the Midwestern heartland. As Carl Van Doren insisted in the *Nation* that year, Edgar Lee Masters, Sinclair Lewis, and Sherwood Anderson were, in effect, rejecting through revolt the Midwestern villages of their beginnings, as well as the culture and mores of their youth, as they sought a richer, more sophisticated urban fulfillment.
>
> So attractive was this critical view to many who either had fled the Midwest, as had Van Doren, or had never known it, that "the revolt from the village" became the most widespread and most widely accepted literary metaphor of the Midwest. ("Sherwood Anderson and the Critics," p. 1)

7. Studies that focus on *Winesburg, Ohio* as a narrative of isolation and failure, in contrast to my emphasis, are represented by Stouck, "*Winesburg, Ohio*, and the Failure of Art" and "*Winesburg, Ohio*, as a Dance of Death," and Fussell, "*Winesburg, Ohio*: Art and Isolation."
8. For discussions of women in Anderson, see Bunge, "Women in Sherwood Anderson's Fiction," and Atlas, "Sherwood Anderson and the Women of Winesburg."
9. William R. Robinson's "The Imagination of Skin" focuses on the importance of

skin in one medium—the movies—but his stimulating ideas could be applied to other media as well.

10. Chris Browning has also noted Kate Swift's creative, physical influence on both Hartman and Willard. See Browning's "Kate Swift: Sherwood Anderson's Creative Eros."

11. For a very different reading of "Loneliness," see Pickering, "*Winesburg, Ohio*: A Portrait of the Artist."

CHAPTER 4

1. For biographical information on Hemingway, I am using Baker's *Ernest Hemingway: A Life Story*.

2. Wesley A. Kort sums up the problem: "The subjection of the texts to the context occurs so often, of course, because of the undeniable and controversial character of the author. . . . The narrative texts are used to illustrate a point or make a case about the man" ("Human Time in Hemingway's Fiction," p. 579).

3. Carlos Baker, for example, probably the most influential scholar of Hemingway's life and work and the only critic to examine patterns in *Green Hills of Africa*, often does not get the title right, referring to *The Green Hills of Africa*—not a minor point, as I later point out. Moreover, it is all but impossible to find a reader who does more than politely dismiss the book. Many are not even polite. Some early reviewers found *Green Hills* "relatively meaningless," "trivial," "a disappointment" (Wagner, *Ernest Hemingway: A Reference Guide*, pp. 35–37). Later critics spoke of it as a book in which Hemingway "loses his mastery" (Moloney, "Ernest Hemingway: The Missing Third Dimension," p. 189); "one of his poorer books" (Carpenter, *American Literature and the Dream*, p. 185). In 1964, Stanley Hyman declared *A Moveable Feast* Hemingway's most insignificant book, "worse than *Green Hills of Africa* (*New Leader* 47 [May 11, 1964]: 8)." In 1968, Richard Hovey called *Green Hills* "a minor piece that does not deserve to last" (*Hemingway: The Inward Terrain*, p. 112). And later critics—Chaman Nahal (1971), Floyd Watkins (1977), Wirt Williams (1981), and James Nagel (1984)—either do not mention it or quickly pass on to other things.

4. My interest in Nick's vitality and movement contrasts with other approaches. William Bysshe Stein states that "with the sole exception of 'Big Two-Hearted River,' the adventures of Hemingway's Nick Adams are a chronicle of sterile egoism" ("Ritual in Hemingway's 'Big Two-Hearted River,'" p. 555). Robert Evans believes that "as early as 1925, with *In Our Time*, Hemingway had discovered how important it is not to think" ("Hemingway and the Pale Cast of Thought," p. 165). One of several studies to discuss *In Our Time* as a unified work is Burhans, "The Complex Unity of *In Our Time*."

5. For a different response to this story, see Paul Victor Anderson, "Nick's Story in Hemingway's 'Big Two-Hearted River.'" Anderson says that Nick "flees to a situation where he hopes to be insulated from thoughts that remind him of his personal shortcomings and also from actions in which he would fail and thereby destroy the little self-confidence he has left" (p. 565).

6. I regard *Green Hills* as the product of an act of the imagination. Most critics, however, see it strictly in biographical terms. See, for example, Motola, "Hemingway's Code," and Baker, *Hemingway: The Writer as Artist*. Baker says that "the necessity of achieving verisimilitude is common to both fiction and non-fiction. So is the challenge of working out a reasonably tight architectural structure. . . . Yet if one compares the book with such novels as *A Farewell to Arms* and *For Whom the Bell Tolls*, the lower stature of *The* [sic] *Green Hills* is evident enough" (p. 167).

It is worth noting that in the text of *Green Hills* it is only the character Kandisky who attaches the label "Hemingway" to the narrator and that the narrator himself is creating a persona.

7. In this statement and the next two paragraphs, I am indebted to what is throughout an insightful discussion of *Green Hills* by Susan Lynn Drake. See her unpublished dissertation, "The Inward Journey: Shape and Pattern in *Green Hills of Africa*." Scholes and Kellogg, *The Nature of Narrative*, p. 98.

8. "It was into the design of useful things that these people inevitably turned the universal creative instinct. . . . The men and women who built a civilization in the American wilderness had to relearn a truth which many of their European contemporaries had been able to get along without: the truth of function" (Kouwenhoven, *Made in America*, p. 16). "As Joseph Wood Krutch once remarked, Europeans learned to use the machine as a middle-aged man learns to drive a car—dubiously and without ceasing to feel that it is alien to his nature; but Americans took to it with the enthusiasm of youth and manipulated its levers as if they were muscles of their own bodies" (ibid., p. 214).

CHAPTER 5

1. Consequently, I do not find it useful to compare *The Big Sky* to eastern works focusing on character development. Richard Astro, however, approaches the book in those terms:

> And Huck Finn on and near the Mississippi, Ishmael on the *Pequod*, and Hester Prynne in Salem grow to a consciousness *in society* as the conflicts and contradictions are resolved, however indefinite those resolutions must be. They become fully-developed, multi-dimensional characters who share the complicated needs, the acute problems of us all, and who make the adjustments and adaptations necessary for a full and meaningful life.
>
> But in Western wilderness novels, particularly in those set in the times just before the closing of the frontier, a final resolution of the conflict is impossible, because the physical conditions necessary for that resolution do not exist. The best wilderness novelists—A. B. Guthrie, Vardis Fisher and Frederick Manfred—can create exciting plots . . . But because their characters are cut-off and alone, by choice deprived of the kind of meaningful social contact which leads one from innocence to experience, they are limited by their medium. In short, the wilderness novel simply cannot transcend its occasion. ("*The Big Sky* and the Limits of Wilderness Fiction," p. 113).

2. The actual existence of the world toward which Boone moves distinguishes the western novel from such eastern works as Irving's "Rip Van Winkle" or Updike's *Rabbit, Run*, where the alternative to everyday life is simply fantasy. However, a central characteristic of western writing is its depiction of the reality of the alternative—the West.

3. "Indeed Boone's greatest weakness in his perception of the external world is precisely this inability to assess the magnitude of change. For him the world exists in a constant idyllic present, and though he sees it alter around him he refuses to recognize its transformation" (Folsom, *The American Western Novel*, p. 68).

CHAPTER 6

1. "This combination of the intellectual and the West is essential to an understanding of Walter Van Tilburg. To ignore either side, or the tension between the two, or to think of him as a 'natural' Westerner who wrote *The Ox-Bow Incident* and was then made too critically conscious by academia . . . or to call Clark an anti-

intellectual is to oversimplify. He did grow up in the West, and nothing is more important to him than land and its meanings . . . but his youth and his family were characterized as much by an atmosphere of sophisticated learning as by a love of nature" (Westbrook, *Walter Van Tilburg Clark*, p. 24).

2. Smith, *Virgin Land*, p. 188.

3. The earliest reviews of Clark's first novel took this approach, whose hold continues to be felt even in such standard studies of western writing as Folsom's *The American Western Novel* (pp. 124–25) and Milton's *The Novel of the American West*, wherein Milton writes, "It is not the lynching itself that is important but the motives and pressures . . . which lead to the lynching or allow it to happen. What causes injustice?" (p. 207).

4. Art Croft is usually discussed as an observer, a Greek chorus figure, who functions only indirectly in the action. "Art Croft's function as narrator prevents him from taking the side of good to which his nature seems to incline him" (Portz, "Idea and Symbol in Walter Van Tilburg Clark," p. 122); "the arguments of Davies exceed Croft's poor powers of comprehension (poor in precisely the sense that any mere mortal's powers are poor)" (Cochran, "Nature and the Nature of Man in *The Ox-Bow Incident*," p. 260). See also Anderson, "Character Portrayal in *The Ox-Bow Incident*."

5. I wish to distinguish between the presentation of Art Croft (and Art itself) as a figure watching the action from outside and the failure of Art/Art to accept an active role within the group by withdrawing into the role of observer. Donald E. Houghton's essay, "The Failure of Speech in *The Ox-Bow Incident*," is particularly stimulating on the potential of Art/Art. Houghton argues that Croft fundamentally distrusts language: "Croft shares with the other men a distrust of language and he looks askance at those who use it easily and well. . . . Croft's inability or unwillingness to enter into exchanges with those who attempt to put into words their views concerning the moral and legal aspects of what is being planned reveals something basic about Croft and his kind which contributes importantly to the tragic event at the Ox-Bow" (p. 1247). Houghton seems to suggest that the necessary role of the narrator is not as observer but as one who can find language and form that will work in these new conditions.

6. Max Westbrook sees Clark's novel as one that explores the implications of man alienated against himself: "[Osgood] has given himself over to officialdom's grotesque separation of man from the totality to which he belongs. He has alienated himself from that essential unity of thought and things—and truncated man is a disgusting sight to behold. This alienation, I think, explains why Clark began the novel with a brief study in restoration. Though close friends, Art and Gil have succumbed to the tension of winter range, and they have argued and fought. They must now ease out of their divisive feelings, but the restoration can take place only if there is a sense of balance, a sense of the whole" ("The Archetypal Ethic of *The Ox-Bow Incident*," p. 113).

In these terms, the unifying role of Art can be seen as centrally important. See also Wilner's "Walter Van Tilburg Clark": "Nevada makes man lonely. It does so very literally, but it does so metaphysically as well. If man is forced to tolerate his own company, he is also obliged to scrutinize it. If he finds within himself all the oppositions of a larger society, he might also discover how inner peace is achieved through a harmony of these oppositions. He may learn also that his life—his own point in space—is only a minute and temporary arrangement in a much larger and more fixed proposition" (p. 103). It is that loneliness that such writers as Clark, Austin, and Waters see as needing the healing act of a unifying perceiver.

Extending these ideas in his book, *Walter Van Tilburg Clark*, Westbrook develops the religious element in Clark's writing: "In this sense of the word, Walter Van Tilburg Clark is religious, a sacred man in the twentieth-century. He meets [Mircea] Eliade's definition, specifically, in that he believes 'that nothing can begin, nothing can be *done*, without a previous orientation,' and that a sacred view of space is the only possible ground of orientation" (p. 23).

7. See Cochran, "Nature and the Nature of Man in *The Ox-Bow Incident*," p. 262, and Milton, *The Novel of the American West*, p. 198.

CHAPTER 7

1. See, for example, Milton's *The Novel of the American West* and Pilkington's *Harvey Fergusson*.

2. Jehlen discusses this topic in *American Incarnation*.

CHAPTER 8

1. Morris, *About Fiction*, p. 11.

2. Critics are divided in their perception of the underlying thrust of Morris's work. On the one hand, many consider the dominant force in his writing to be nostalgia, even an Eliotic "still point"; see, for example, J. C. Wilson, "Wright Morris and the Search for the 'Still Point,' " and Wydeven, "Consciousness Refracted." Gail Crump, on the other hand, stresses dynamics in Morris and contrasts his views to those of Wayne Booth and David Madden, whom he describes as tending "to treat transcendence in itself as an unalloyed good" (*The Novels of Wright Morris*, p. 9).

Morris has commented in an interview that nostalgia is a starting point from which the individual moves forward.

> Nostalgia, the past, which I first had to rediscover as a matter of personal self-discovery, can be traced in the novels, I think. First the infatuation with the past, a conviction that the past was real and desirable, and should be the way life is. Then a somewhat scrutinous and skeptical attitude toward the past. After which the present begins to come into the picture. . . . Then the past begins to be questioned, and over a period of eight novels, the past first dominated, then was compelled to recede. . . . In a way my books show a development of an escape from nostalgia. (Bleufarb, "Point of View," p. 45)

See also Waterman, "The Novels of Wright Morris."

3. Morris, *The Territory Ahead*, pp. 19, 25.

4. Because of its interesting use of the photo-text technique, *The Home Place* is frequently discussed by scholars, who seem to agree that the book is one of Morris's weaker efforts. I refer in particular to Alan Trachtenberg, who writes that "one weakness of this book is that the pictures, which are all direct and straightforward, with an occasional close-up, compete with the narrative for our attention. Seeing them on alternate pages of the text, we cannot always experience them and the narrative simultaneously" ("The Craft of Vision," p. 46); to David Madden, who states that "although the photographs are excellent, their relation to the text is more literal and less interesting than in *The Inhabitants*" (*Wright Morris*, p. 52); and to Gail Crump, who says that the novel "does demonstrate Morris's increasing insight into his past, but the insight is evidenced only on the conceptual level, not in mastery of his fictional technique" (*The Novels of Wright Morris*, p. 57).

I disagree with such readings. The divisive, static world established by the photo-text technique is precisely the problem with which Clyde Muncy's imagination has to deal. More helpful, I think, is Mary Ann Flood's Master's thesis, "The Hero-Witness Relationship in the Fiction of Wright Morris" (1971).

5. About Jubal Gainer, Morris says, "I see him as a rather ordinary, ignorant, open-ended American juvenile. He has an opportunity to do what we think of as irrational. I consider him absolutely normal and his seeming psychopathic elements are introduced by the options within his situations. . . . The situation creates the violence. He is not violence-prone at all. He is merely another young man on a motorcycle, full of beans, and he's young, and he's ignorant, and outside of that he's Huck Finn" (*Conversations with Wright Morris*, p. 30).

6. Gail Crump offers a different description of the book's intriguing structure: "The image of orbiting brings together both transcendence (being out of this world) and immanence (being in motion through space-time), and the book's structure—nine brief chapters following Jubal's frenetic rampage through Picket— suggests the motion of the open road, while opening and closing the book with almost identical framing passages suggests the completion of an orbit" (*The Novels of Wright Morris*, p. 186).

CHAPTER 9

1. Doig's commitment to family and relationships is perhaps suggested by his dedication in *This House of Sky*. Doig says, "Westward we go free," an interesting variation of Thoreau's statement, "Westward I go free."

2. Doig, *News*, pp. 144,22.

3. Tanner, "Notes for a Comparison between American and European Romanticism," p. 150, and Tocqueville, *Democracy in America*, 2:3–4.

CHAPTER 10

1. To Ford, as to Francis Parkman and most eastern imaginations, the West is less important in itself than in its purpose of reminding how much wilderness needs shaping along traditional civilizing lines. John Baxter, in *The Cinema of John Ford*, says of Ford's cavalry films that "the subject of all these films is seldom the cavalry but rather the order of community life placed in conflict with an opposing destructive force" (p. 79). Andrew Sinclair describes Ford's vision of American history as being shown in the opening sequences of Abraham Lincoln in *The Iron Horse*: "With the father of the nation supporting Manifest Destiny, the building of the railroad to link the United States can be presented as a mission of strong men and iron machines against the resistance of the wilderness and the Indian tribes standing in their way" (*John Ford*, p. 35). Jim Kitses's brief statement in *Horizons West* indicates the inevitable problem created when a viewer is less interested in the object itself than in what it can be made to represent: "The peak comes in the forties when Ford's works are bright monuments to his vision of the trek of the faithful to the Promised Land, the populist hope of an ideal community. . . . But as the years slip by . . . we find a regret for the past, a bitterness at the larger role of Washington, and a desolation over the neglect of older values" (p. 13).

2. Discussing the setting in *Stagecoach*, John Baxter describes Ford's handling of scene: "Ford's style is perfectly mirrored in this landscape, the measured flow of his theme in the flat plain, its dramatic peaks in the sudden eruptions of stone around which he always sets his major battles and dramatic confrontations, while his concept of society, in which man, orderly and respectful of rules, maintains the natural order in the shadow of unassailable principles, seems emblematised in his films of the cavalry fighting and dying among the valley's stones while overhead the omnipresent clouds suggest a higher reality of mind and of the spirit to which all are subservient" (*The Cinema of John Ford*, p. 71).

3. In Ford, says Andrew Sinclair, "the Apache typify the wild forces of nature

and nemesis"; against "the outer chaos of dying and war and wilderness" stand ritual, law, and the Catholic Church, which "guarded the soul as the American navy guarded the shores" (*John Ford*, pp. 81, 133, 135).

4. "The west was his peacetime nostalgia," according to Andrew Sinclair, who sees the postwar *My Darling Clementine* as "a western about the adjustment of natural outsiders to the rule of law and church and family" (*John Ford*, p. 129). This adjustment is enforced by the protective arm of the cavalry in the movies of the late 1940s.

5. Robert Ray has a fine discussion of this technique in *A Certain Tendency of the Hollywood Cinema, 1930–1980*, pp. 229–37.

6. " 'What a name for a heavy!' [Lee] Marvin said of Liberty Valance. 'I never got over it! Liberty is a dangerous dangerous thing. It requires more discipline than anything else' " (Sinclair, *John Ford*, p. 195).

7. Kitses, *Horizons West*, p. 159.

8. Seydor, *Peckinpah*, p. 40.

9. A fine study of *Ride the High Country*, *The Ballad of Cable Hogue*, and *Convoy* is Marshall, "Within the Moral Eye—Peckinpah's Art of Visual Narration."

10. Jim Kitses, for example, sums up the movie by focusing on Gil Westrum and Steve Judd: "Discussion of this great work has often erred in relegating the Scott figure [Gil Westrum] to a secondary role. . . . But these two heroes, like Dundee and Tyreen, are masks for the same face, expressions of the same spirit, the spirit of the American West. Judd and Westrum, judge and cowboy, vision and violence, Peckinpah insists that both were necessary in a savage land" (*Horizons West*, pp. 159–60). According to Paul Seydor, "The theme is diminishment, disillusion, and compromise" (*Peckinpah*, p. 33).

11. Seydor, *Peckinpah*, p. 32.

12. Sinclair has noted that father figures and the authority associated with them are central in Ford's movies (*John Ford*, p. 35). In contrast, father figures inevitably die or are absent in Peckinpah's movies. Peckinpah's are stories of young people transforming their fathers' values and discovering their own way.

13. Both Seydor and Kitses concentrate on the problems of making *Major Dundee*; in spite of those problems, Peckinpah's imagination dominates the movie, and it becomes "the story of a company divided against itself" (Seydor, *Peckinpah*, p. 55). For McKinney, "The problem is in determining who the enemy is" (*Sam Peckinpah*, p. 64).

14. Peckinpah's interest in images contrasts sharply with Ford's. As several scholars have noted, Ford's movies deny individuality. Because he is primarily concerned with the truth, as he understands it, about country and law, Ford's genius lies in taking stereotypes and creating archetypes (Sinclair, *John Ford*, p. 22). "Characters in Ford's films work under a strong disadvantage; deprived of individuality in favour of embodying the virtues of a society, they are types rather than people, and as they cannot alter without casting doubt on the virtues they represent, their personalities remain frozen in time" (Baxter, *The Cinema of John Ford*, p. 19). The continuing use of John Wayne, for example, creates what is recognized worldwide as the archetypal westerner. Peckinpah, however, finds within each new image its special qualities. When John Wayne rides on camera, the audience *knows* (rather than *sees*) what to expect from his character. Not so with William Holden in *The Wild Bunch* or Jason Robards in *Cable Hogue*: we have to focus on the event that is each character to see the story being told.

15. The centrality of the individual is made clear in Cable's early speech: "It's Cable Hogue talkin' . . . Hogue . . . me . . . Cable Hogue . . . Hogue . . . me . . . me . . . I did it . . . Cable Hogue . . . I found it . . . me." In the course of the movie, Cable will find other individuals and begin to relate to them.